FREEFORM P

Design and Creation of Original Wearable Art Jewelry

Karen Williams

Skunk Hill Studio

All text, illustrations, artwork, editing and layout produced by Karen Williams unless otherwise noted.

Photo credits JFH taken by Joseph Heck - thanks for all of your support and assistance with this project! It wouldn't have happened without you.

ISBN-10: 144998052X

SKUNK HILL STUDIO
Seattle, Washington
www.skunkhillstudio.com, skunkhillstudio@yahoo.com

Contents

Creativity & Inspiration

Nature - a powerful source of inspiration.

To create one's world in any of the arts takes courage. – Georgia O'Keefe

We can all be creative. Great artists make the task of creation look easy as they seemingly pull imagery out of thin air. In truth, the work of most artists is based upon considerable focused study: training their inner eye to truly see; training their minds to remember; learning through experimentation what they want to say in their work and how to express it in their chosen medium. Creativity is less an inborn trait than a set of skills that can be developed.

By the time we reach adulthood, most of us have spent a dozen or more years in school, studying a wide range of subjects. It's hard to remember where we began, how we had to learn to hold the pencil correctly before we could begin to learn to write. We learned through practice, study, trial and error, and play. However, few schools provide formal training in art or design. So is it any wonder if our creative talents are less developed than many of our other skills? I am astonished by how many people I meet in my workshops who are utterly convinced that they can never be creative, yet are courageous enough to make the attempt, regardless. If this sounds familiar, then I ask you to give yourself some time to develop the necessary skills. They are skills, you can learn them; everyone can be creative.

At its essence, Creativity is a willingness to pay attention and ask questions, and the courage to experiment with the answers. To be creative we must hone our powers of observation, learning to truly see our surroundings. Understanding some of the basic principles of design will enable us to analyze and interpret what we see. And, in the case of freeform (sometimes called sculptural) peyote, we must master some basic mechanical skills involving a modicum of hand-eye coordination. Combine these three and you're ready to turn inspiration into unique objects of art and craft. Oh, and it helps to have a sense of adventure - a willingness to ask "what if" and see what happens.

This book is arranged in much the way I think about the creative process. It all starts with an idea. Sometimes finding the initial idea is the hardest part. Once you have your inspiration, it's time to choose the materials that best express that idea. In this book, I'll share information about some of my favorite beads and findings and discuss my chosen 'tools of the trade.' I've divided the stitching chapter up into several sections including basic peyote stitches, freeform peyote, and finishing techniques. Look through the entire chapter before you start stitching; freeform peyote is an organic, continually evolving art form, offering surprises and asking 'what-if' as you work. The more you know, the more you have to draw from, making the evolution a far less painful process.

Finding Inspiration

In her fantastic book, *The Artist's Way*, Julia Cameron likens creativity to a well. Before you can draw from the well, you need to make sure there's 'water' and prime the pump. Your well of creativity is filled with images, thoughts, feelings, objects and ideas. They can be fun, frivolous, riveting, beautiful, playful, heart-rending, inspiring, terrible, or any number of other adjectives - the only real requirement is that they speak to you.

Ask yourself questions. What imagery are you drawn to? Do you love details or the big picture, portraits or landscapes, still-lives or cityscapes? What colors? Are they subtle or bold? Why?

Give yourself permission to bring home bits and pieces that catch your eye or delight your senses. If you don't already have one, find a place to display and enjoy your treasures.

There are no wrong answers! Think of yourself as a reporter or a private investigator. All the while, you're filling your creative well and building a personal library of reference points.

Working with Design

Collecting ideas and beginning sketches for a series of work based upon an ocean theme.

Freeform peyote is an abstract, organic art form based upon color, value, texture and line; each piece a unique creation unsuited to specific instructions or patterns. Success in this medium relies heavily upon your comfort and facility in making the final design decisions as you stitch. However, those decisions should be based upon a solid foundation. The elements of design are tools you can use to help translate and distill inspiration into a finished piece and guide your stitching.

Explore your inspiration as discrete components of visual information, studying each element separately. Determine which are essential to your interpretation and of greatest impact. Experiment to better understand how changes affect your perception of the whole. The better you understand the underlying design elements in your inspiration, the easier it will be to convey them in your work.

Design Elements

Gradations of value from high (white) to low (black).

Compositions with different proportions of value. Note the extended value range in five of the six examples.

Value and Value Keys

Value is a measurement of lightness or darkness. It can be measured absolutely - against a scale where white is always the highest value and stygian black the lowest. But in between the two extremes lie myriad shades of grey, and value is the way we judge their relative lightness or darkness in comparison with one another.

Taken as a whole, the values of all the elements in a particular piece make up its value key. When an object catches our eye, we respond first to its value key, then to other visual information such as its color. That initial response helps establish our emotional reaction to the object. Understanding how people react to differing value keys allows you to anticipate those reactions and to better control their response, reinforcing the intended message of your piece.

While everyone reacts to value slightly differently, works composed of lighter values - such as pastels - tend to evoke delicate, atmospheric, soft, or romantic emotions and are usually considered more feminine or childlike.

Compositions of darker values are often seen as more masculine: the hunter green library with its dark walnut shelves. Such compositions may seem theatrical, mysterious, or even depressing depending upon the colors chosen.

Many bead and fabric artists seem to be particularly drawn to the mid-range, where all their values are neither very light nor very dark. Colors in this mid-range can be quite bold and rich, reflecting both sunlight and mystery.

Works composed entirely of closely related values such as those described above photograph nicely in color, but are often quite boring, lacking visual interest, if photographed in black and white due to their low value contrast.

Increasing the contrast by using a wider range of values can increase the visual interest and extend the emotional range of the piece. With an extended value range, try varying the proportion of light, dark and mid value elements. The dominant value - think percentages of the surface here - most heavily flavors the emotional tone of the piece, but can be tempered by contrasting values. A splash of darker color can wake an otherwise pastel piece from its quiet slumber, as can a shot of light into the darkness of a low value composition. When a design seems bland, increasing the value range may provide the needed spice.

Study your inspiration to understand its value range. Look for the highs and lows; how light and how dark does it go? How wide is its value range? What are the dominant values? Play with varying the proportions of different values from light to dark to find compositions that appeal to you.

The same quilt block in 4 value keys, both in black & white and in color. Top to bottom by rows: High, Middle, Low and Extended Value Keys. Note the value contrast is far greater in the bottom blocks.

Source photos for color palette for "Autumn Glory" bracelet.

Working with Color

Color theory fascinates me - why certain combinations looks so right, while others fail to quite make the mark. To my mind, color is one of the most satisfying places to start a freeform peyote design.

It can be tempting to simply dive in and begin stitching; however it pays to remember that even the smallest projects, such as a ring or pair of earrings, will involve several hours of work.

In my experience, when a finished piece doesn't quite hit the mark, the problem is almost always color related. I've seen this both in my own and in my students' work. It's a good reason to spend a little time studying how colors interact.

Understanding the relationships in your color choices improves your confidence in your decisions and the final product. I begin most bracelets and other smaller projects with a clear idea of my color scheme and use the other elements of design to help me tweak my choices for maximum impact. The larger the project, the more time I'm willing to spend in the design stage, considering it an investment in the finished project.

My bracelet, "Autumn Glory", started with several photographs of Virginia creeper in full fall color almost obscuring a brick apartment building. I loved the juxtaposition of the blazing red and orange leaves against the dark green/brown vines and the battered red brick. The thick vines and trailing leaves also provided strong elements of line and texture which I could easily adapt to suit as I stitcheds.

The Language of Color

Intensity. All three reds are the same basic value, converted to black & white they are the same shade of grey, but the true red has the highest/strongest intensity. The lower the intensity, the more the color seems to fade into the background.

Intensity. Called saturation in the printing world, intensity refers to the relative strength and purity of a color. Primary colors are fully intense examples of their basic hues. Dusty rose is considerably less intense than its cousin, primary red.

More intense colors are generally perceived as "brighter" and tend to be seen as open, positive, bold, while less intense colors and compositions can be mysterious, subtle, depressing or insipid, depending upon the exact combinations and the viewer.

Undertones. Three blues with different undertones. The middle blue has a warm (red) undertone. The last blue has a cool (green) undertone.

Color Temperature. Every hue and every color has a relative warmth or coolness which is its color temperature. The red-to-yellow color families are described as 'warm', while the green-to-violet spectrum is considered 'cool'. Orange is the hottest color and blue is the coldest while yellow-green and red-violet sit on the cusps between warm and cool.

Undertones. Variations in the undertones of a particular hue creates temperature differences even within a single color family. Think of fire engine red versus fuschia. Fire engine red is hot because of its warm orange undertones, while fuschia, though eye-popping, appears much cooler with its blue undertones. It's often easiest to identify these undertones by comparing several colors of the same hue as in the example at right.

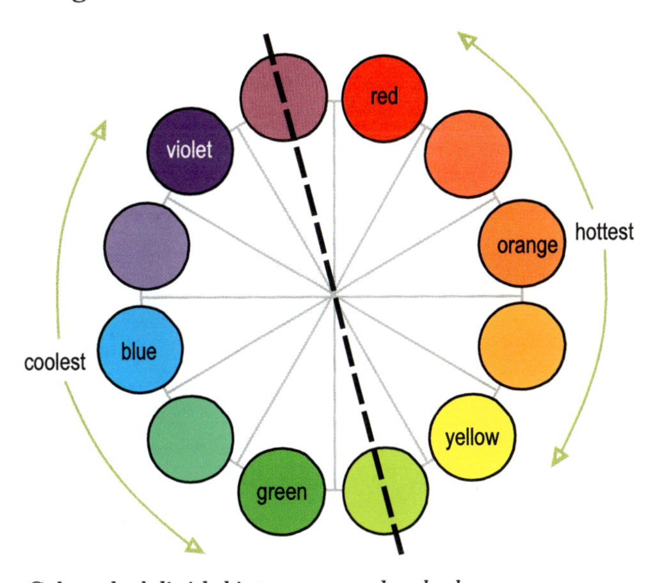

Color wheel divided into warm and cool colors.

Color Temperature. The yellow-green appears cool when surrounded by warmer colors in the top example. The same yellow-green seems much warmer when surrounded by cooler colors in the bottom sample.

Relative Temperature. In a composition, our perception of a color's temperature is affected by the temperatures of its neighbors. A moderately cool color will appear much cooler if it is surrounded by other, warmer colors than if it is surrounded by cooler tones. Red-violet and yellow-green show the greatest temperature changes based upon their surroundings because they lie on the cusp between the warm and cool hues, making it easier for them to tip in either direction. Thus, a red-violet is comparatively cool when grouped with reds and oranges, but becomes considerably warmer when grouped with blues and greens.

Perceived Depth or Push/Pull. I often use variations in color temperature as highlights or accents in my work. Temperature variations create a push/pull effect where warm colors seem to advance while cooler colors recede in a composition. Because of this, you can use color temperature to help push elements into the background or pull them to the foreground.

Push/Pull effect based upon color temperatures and value. Warmer, lighter colors advance, cooler, darker colors recede.

The effect of value on the perceived intensity of a color. The blue is the exactly the same in all four squares, but our perception of it changes based upon the background. Also note the push/pull effect of value where lighter values seem to advance, pushing darker colors back.

Color Studies

You may find it useful to make a color study before you begin bead selection. The goal of a color study is to isolate and clearly identify the exact colors, intensities and values you plan to incorporate into your final piece.

You can use paints, paint chips, colored papers, yarn, threads, or even beads to create your color study. Whatever you choose to use is simply a means to and end; the key is to have a wide enough range of color samples to be able to match those present in your inspiration. Paint chips are one of my favorite materials; they come in a plethora of colors and the price can't be beat, since they're usually free at larger hardware stores.

Above: two color studies, for my bracelet "Autumn Glory" made from paint chips and wrapped threads.
Top Left: painted paper color study for "Hydrangea Spring."

To do a color study, compare the colors in your inspiration to your samples. When you find a match cut it out or set it aside. Continue until you have found matches for all of the main colors from your inspiration.

If you're using paint swatches, glue or tape them neatly to a piece of paper. If using yarn or threads, try wrapping them around a piece of card stock, securing the ends at the back with a bit of tape. If beads, string them onto a doubled strand of beading thread, using enough of each color to extend 1/4 - 1/2". Use your completed study to help find and match colors during bead selection, including any trips to the bead store.

Building the Color Wheel

The standard color wheel is composed of the three primary colors – red, blue and yellow – alternating with the three secondary colors – orange, purple and green - each created by mixing two primaries. The twelve step color wheel includes tertiary colors produced by mixing a primary with one of its neighboring secondary colors (yellow + green = yellow/ green). This standard color wheel depicts pure, fully intense versions of each color; its purpose to help you better visualize the relationships between these colors.

Why not build your own unique color wheels by uniformly varying the temperature, value or intensity of all the colors? You could generate personalized color wheels based upon any color theme. For instance, you could build a color wheel of pastels where you've lightened the value of each color several steps. A jewel-toned wheel might include darker, but fully intense versions of the colors, while an earth toned wheel would include warmer, more muted (less intense) colors.

In each case, the key is to look for the relationships between your chosen colors to build your unique color wheel. Note that purple is always the darkest (lowest) and yellow the lightest (highest) value in any wheel. Once you have built your custom color wheel, you can use it to develop additional color schemes.

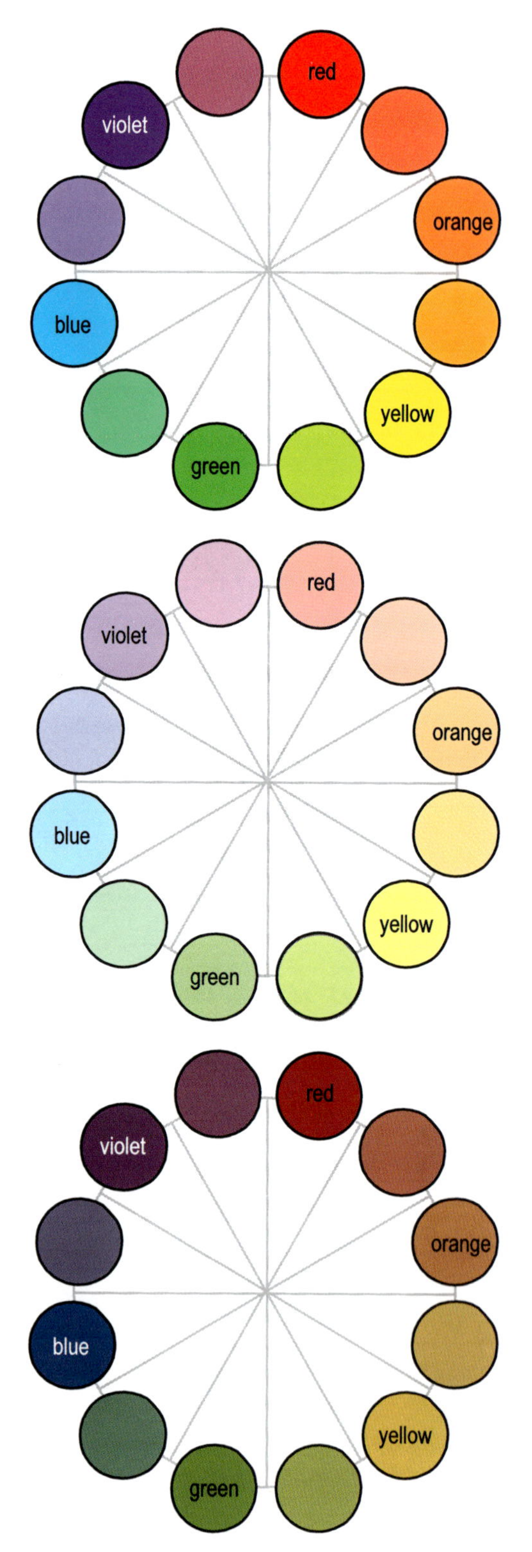

Above from top: Standard 12-step color wheel, custom pastel and earth-tone variations.

Using the Color Wheel

Monochromatic compositions are built around a single color. To increase the visual contrast, incorporate multiple shades or values (*see page 9*) of the same color, from light to dark. Consider varying the color intensities and undertones to increase the composition's visual depth. Strong temperature differences in the undertones may push the color scheme from monochromatic towards analogous.

Analogous colors are next door neighbors on the color wheel. Blue, blue-green and green is one example of an analogous color combination. Analogous colors go together naturally due to their close proximity and tend to be easy on the eye. If the colors you've chosen clash, the problem is likely in their undertones or intensities.

Complimentary colors sit across from each other on the color wheel – red and green for instance. Like the old saying "opposites attract", complimentary colors contrast and enrich each other, creating bold and lively color schemes. If your complimentary color pairing isn't working, the clash is most likely a result of differences in the intensities or undertones. Try evaluating the problem by asking yourself if they would sit comfortably on the same color wheel.

Split complimentary compositions use the neighbors to either side of one half of a complimentary pairing, as in the example - purple, yellow-orange and yellow-green.

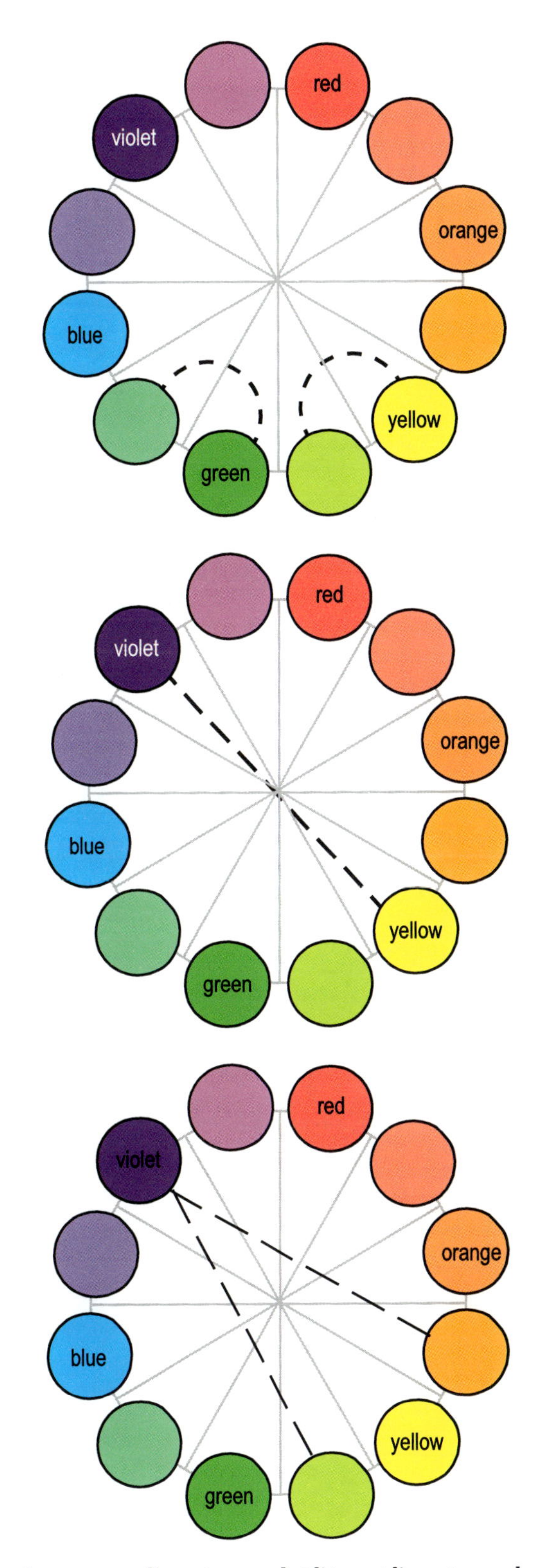

Analagous, complimentary and split complimentary colors

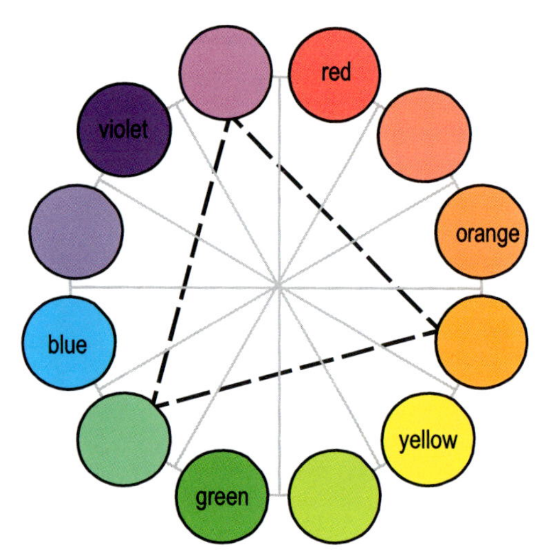

Triadic color combinations based upon the color wheel.

Triadic colors or Triads are three colors evenly spaced around the color wheel. Triads create lively but more balanced compositions with strong contrasts between all three elements. The primary triad - red, yellow, blue - is often associated with the bold vibrancy of children's toys. More subtle combinations can be created using the secondary or tertiary colors. As with complimentary colors, pay careful attention to the intensities and undertones when developing triadic compositions.

Texture and Line

With freeform peyote you will work with both visual and physical textures. Physical texture can be felt. Each bead has a physical texture which may be smooth, rough, bumpy, ridged, etc. In addition, each bead has a visual texture which may be matte, shiny, metallic, iridescent, etc. In most cases, this texture cannot be felt physically, but visually presents a variety of surfaces.

As you create your freeform peyote, you will combine your beads into additional textures of pattern and line. Smoothly interlocking sections of peyote stitch form a repeating pattern framework for more organic alterations and encrustations. Lines of beads forming bridges, ridges, and arches help move color from section to section, supporting your design theme, and directing the eye around the piece. Accent and focal beads provide additional variety in shape, size and texture.

Texture and line from the forest floor.

Principles of Design

At their very simplest, the principles of design provide a practical means of defining and manipulating the relationships between the various design elements in your work. In his book ***Design is Where You Find It***, Orville K. Chatt succinctly describes the design principles:

> **Unity**: a quality of oneness
> **Rhythm**: a quality of movement
> **Balance**: a quality of equilibrium
> **Proportion**: a relationship of part
> **Opposition**: a quality of contrast
> **Variety**: a quality of variation

Decorated papers and a beaded amulet bag echo the colors of the rainforest.

Balance and Contrast

Similarities are pleasing to the eye and provide respite, but too much similarity breeds boredom. Contrast has an energizing effect but, introduce too much contrast and chaos ensues. In developing your design you need to strike a balance between unity and contrast. For instance, if you are working with a very limited color palette, you might use a wider value range to increase the contrast. The limited palette provides a strong unifying element to your design while the wider value range adds visual contrast.

Be wary of balancing all of the elements too carefully. In working with design, think in terms of thirds or fifths instead of halves. If all of the various elements are too carefully balanced, the work will seem bland. While initially pleasing to the eye, a perfectly balanced composition is static and lacks energy. Some elements must necessarily dominate the composition or your work will lack a visual focal point.

Try choosing the dominant colors or values, first. Working from there, include small doses of contrasting elements; too many may seem chaotic or disorganized.

Developing More Complex Projects

While freeform peyote is rewarding, it is not fast, and larger projects such as a collar or covered vessel are likely to take many hours and days of stitching to complete. If you are going to invest that much time in a project, it is worthwhile to do some additional planning up front.

Take a little time to test and develop your ideas. By clarifying what it is you hope to create you will substantially increase the odds that you'll be pleased with the final product.

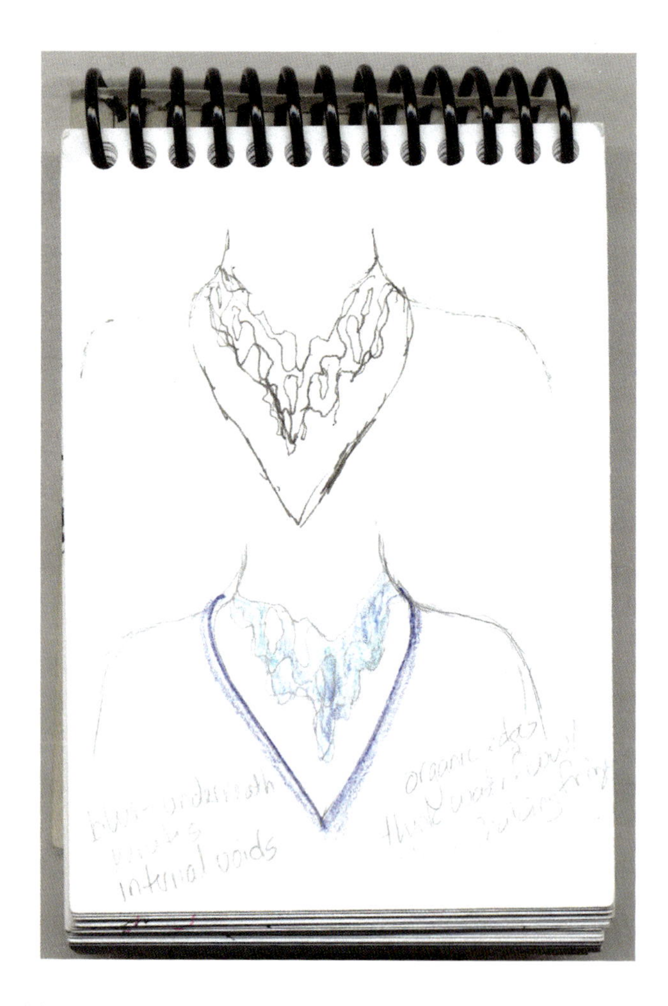

Two sketches for a collar with a water theme. I wanted to play with line, color, and the collar's general size and mass in relation to the neckline of the garment it was made to accompany.

Sketching Ideas

I like to start by making a rough sketch or two of my idea. The sketch needn't be elaborate; include however much or little detail as seems necessary to you. With jewelry, I often sketch it as it might appear on a model. Don't worry about your drawing ability; these sketches are for your eyes only. Their purpose is to help you visualize the piece you want to create.

As you sketch remember that the design does not need to be symmetrical. In fact, asymmetrical designs work better with the organic nature of freeform peyote, so use that to your advantage.

Use these sketches to experiment with color movement and the placement of focal beads. If you have access to a copier (or scanner/printer) start with a black and white drawing and make several copies of your sketch. Color these copies using colored pencils, crayons or markers. This lets you experiment with minimal additional effort.

Measure Your Subject

When creating jewelry for a specific person, I recommend taking some basic measurements to help insure that the piece actually fits them when it's complete. It can be particularly embarrassing if your finished piece is too large or too small for the intended recipient (don't ask me how I know!).

Remember to take into account wearing ease and any overlap necessary for the closure. For instance, with bracelets I add about a half to an inch wearing ease to the wrist circumference in addition to whatever overlap is required by the closure.

A lot depends upon your stitch habits - some techniques shorten the overall length more than others, so you'll want to check periodically as you stitch to make sure the piece still fits.

For a necklace or collar, you will need the neck circumference, a straight line measurement from one side of their neck to the other and the drop length measured from the hollow at the base of their neck to their cleavage (or however low/high the necklace is supposed to go).

For the purposes of measure taking, I differentiate between a collar, necklace and choker thus: a collar has a bib-like shape covering much of the upper chest; a necklace more closely resembles a rope or ribbon and its length is more variable; while a choker fits snuggly around the neck.

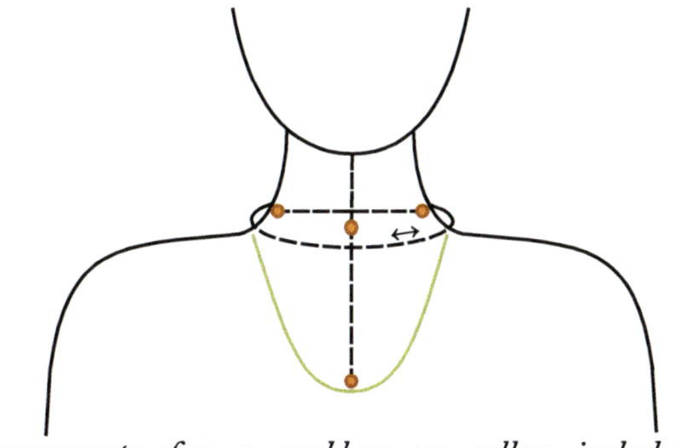

Measurements for a necklace or collar include neck circumference, front drop and front width. Add neck height for a choker.

Measurements for Jewelry

Collar

- Neck Circumference _____
- Neck Width (front) _____
- Drop Length _____

Choker

- Neck Circumference _____
- + Overlap for Closure _____
- + Wearing Ease _____

  Total Circumference _____
- Neck Height* _____

  **defines maximum height of choker*

Necklace

Neck circumference + (Drop length x 2) + overlap for closure = Necklace length

Bracelet

- Wrist Circumference _____
- + Overlap for Closure _____
- + Wearing Ease _____

  Total Length _____

Patterns & Mock ups

Paper mock ups of collar drawn and cut from paper, using the neck measurements I'd taken earlier for this project. My first attempt - the bottom pattern - fit horrendously, which surprised me.

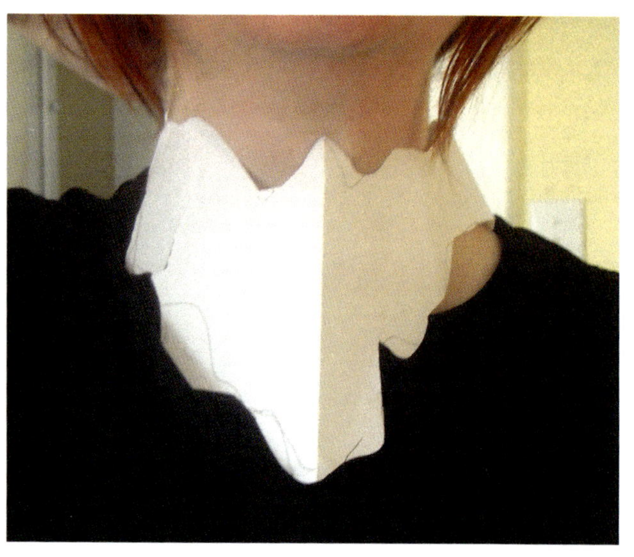

Didn't work! This wasn't going to work - the wide "wings" caused the pattern to ride up around my neck, which was every bit as uncomfortable as it looked. Photo by JFH.

If there are any questions of size or fit, make a full-sized paper mock up of your piece based upon your sketches and measurements. It doesn't need to be complex - just a simple outline of the basic shape. A sheet of typing or legal sized paper is large enough for most projects. You will be surprised how many potential headaches can be eliminated by trying out the basic shape in paper first.

Try the mock up on your model to see how it looks. Are the measurements accurate? Does it aesthetically fill the space intended? If the answer to either of these questions is no, use the mock up to alter the basic size and shape to suit. When you are satisfied, you can also use the mock up as a quick size reference as you stitch.

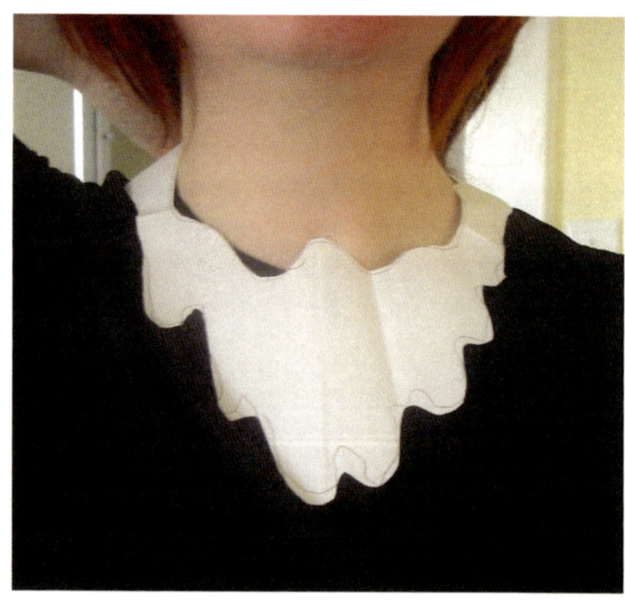

Much better! The bib-like pattern sat right were I wanted it. Photo by JFH.

BEADS AND FINDINGS

In the past ten years the bead market has positively exploded with new and wonderful bead selections. The beads and findings covered in this chapter are some of my favorites, but should be considered no more than the tip of the iceberg of possibilities for suitable materials.

When choosing beads for freeform peyote, it helps to consider the role those beads are going to play in your work. I divide the roles into three main categories: structural, accent and focal.

Structural beads are your basic building blocks, forming the peyote stitch lattice underlying each project. Most of the beads you choose will be in this category. Because structural beads make up the bulk of most projects, they also do the heavy lifting in terms of color.

Consider selecting different surface treatments or finishes – opaque, transparent, matte, metallic – as well. The variety of surface treatments will add to the visual texture of your piece. Use your design inspiration to help guide your bead selection. Remember that thirds or fifths are often more interesting than halves.

Accent beads may or may not form part of the actual structure; either way, their primary role is to provide additional visual or textural interest to the work. If you have a special bead that simply must be a part of the piece; that is your focal bead. All of your other choices should relate back to showcasing that bead.

Structural Beads

Seed, Crow and Pony Beads

Seed beads and their larger cousins, pony or crow beads, make up the bulk of most of my freeform peyote projects. Made from cut pieces of hollow glass canes, most seed beads are smooth with somewhat rounded profiles. They come in several sizes and an amazing array of colors and finishes.

Seed beads are sized in aughts,. The size range runs from 20° to 6°, and may be denoted with a degree mark or a slash and zero (20° or 20/0). The higher the number, the smaller the actual size of the bead. The largest beads (size 6°) are about the size of a coriander seed, while the smallest (size 20°) are not much bigger than a poppy seed. Size 11° is the most common; you will find the widest range of colors and textures in this size. Seed beads are sold strung on hanks (multiple 20" strands tied together) or loose in tubes and plastic bags.

Pony and Crow beads are basically larger seed beads. Both are commonly made of glass, plastic or wood and their names are often used interchangeably. Pony beads come in sizes 5°, 6° and 8°. Technically, crow beads are larger. Their sizes are stated in millimeters: 6mm and 9mm being the most common.

Seed beads are further distinguished by their physical characteristics or country of origin.

Czech beads, also called "rocailles", (pronounced "roh-kai") are widely available at most bead stores. They can be found in sizes 8°, 10°, 11°, 12°, 13° and 14°. Squat and rounded, individual Czech beads tend to be rather irregular in their size and shape. These variations can be used to your advantage in several ways: their irregularities add surface texture; and the size differences make it easier to find just the right beads to fill a particular space.

Charlottes, a rocaille variant, have one to three small flat facets ground onto their surface, giving them their distinctive sparkle, like cut crystal. They are also known as 1-cuts, 2-cuts or 3-cuts depending upon the number of facets.

Japanese beads come in sizes 11° and 15° (equivalent to the Czech size 14°). They tend to be more uniform, with less rounded profiles and generally have larger thread holes than the Czech beads. Because of their larger thread holes, I like to use Japanese beads in "bottleneck" areas where I know I'll have a build up of thread.

Delicas™ are precision manufactured beads known for their very uniform cylindrical shape, thin walls and large thread holes. Prized for loom work where their regularity insures a smooth flat surface, that uniformity is of considerably less importance to freeform peyote. Because they tend to be more expensive than either Czech or Japanese beads, I do not generally use Delicas unless I find a finish and color that I simply cannot resist. That said, if you're looking for a perfectly smooth, uniform surface, you won't go wrong with Delicas.

Comparative sizes of seed beads, from left: 15°, 11°, 8°, 6° and crow beads. Ruler at left for a better sense of scale.

Opposite Page: Bead finishes from top left:
Row 1: gloss opaque, pearlized opaque.
Row 2: matte opaque, transparent gloss.
Row 3 silver-lined transparent charlottes, iridescent semi-transparent.
Row 4: color-lined gloss, matte iridescent semi-transparent.

Right - from left: Size 11° Delicas, Japanese & Czech beads.

Several sizes of bugle beads. Note the twisted bugles at center.

Bugle beads are made from longer pieces of straight or twisted chopped glass cane, with flat and rather blunt ends. Because of this, cheaper bugles often have sharp edges which can saw through your beading thread. For this reason, I can say from sad experience that it's wise to test a couple of beads from a batch before including them in your project.

Drop Shape beads look like rounded teardrops, with an off-center thread hole pushed towards one edge, which is flattened to about half the thickness of the other, rounded half. These are some of my personal favorites, used primarily for accent.

Hexcuts, triangle and rectangular beads are six-sided, three sided and four-sided beads respectively. These beads can be used to interesting effect in the peyote stitch or can be used more sparingly as accent beads.

Clockwise from top left: triangle beads, square cuts, hex beads, drop beads.

I tend to use hex, triangular and bugle beads primarily as accents, however, that is a personal choice. Square beads, for instance could easily replace pony or crow beads in your design.

Bugle Bead Sizes

Size	Inches	Millimeters
1	1/8" (.125)	2.5 mm
2	3/16" (.1875)	5 mm
3	1/4" (.25)	7 mm
4	3/8" (.375)	9 mm
20	3/4" (.75)	20 mm
25	1"	25 mm
30	1.25	30 mm
35	1.375	35 mm
40	1.625	40 mm

Accent and Focal Beads

While the various seed beads do the heavy lifting in forming the structural ground of your work, focal and accent beads should push it up a notch while supporting your design theme. These accents should help tell your design's story.

When considering potential focal points or accents, remember that they don't necessarily have to be beads - I've seen bottle caps, sea glass, miniature pine cones, twigs, sea shells and more used with great success, and used many of these myself. However, with the myriad amazing, beautiful beads available, it would be a shame not to at least consider them.

Lampworked beads by author (hence the imperfections!)

Lampworked beads are created from glass rods heated in an open flame until nearly molten. The hot glass is then wrapped around a stainless steel rod called a mandrel where it is shaped and molded. The surfaces of lampworked beads are often patterned with little glass bumps or colored swirls. Many bead stores sell beautiful, handmade lampworked beads.

Pressed Glass beads are formed by pressing thick molten rods of glass through an automated pressing machine. These beads can take a number of geometric and natural shapes such as diamonds or leaves, and can also be made into small glass charms.

Various pressed glass beads.

Polished stone beads, chips, cabochons and donuts.

Stone and Semi-Precious Gemstone beads are available as chips, rounds, disks, and other geometric and semi-natural shapes. Stone beads give a piece weight, both physically and visually. They tend to have a grounding effect, very different than the specialty glass beads. Irregular gemstone or unpolished chips can have a particularly rough, earthy feel.

Donuts – flat circles with a hole in the center – can be made of a variety of materials, though stone seems to be the most common currently. I personally prefer donuts with a larger center as it makes it easier to work beads through that center without obscuring the hole completely.

Cabochons can be made from a variety of materials including glass, stone and bone. Most cabochons do not have thread holes, so additional steps must be taken to incorporate them into a piece.

They can be captured with netting worked up from the peyote stitch base. Or you can glue a piece of ultrasuede to the flat back of the cabochon using rubber cement. Allow the glue to dry then trim the ultrasuede close to the cabochon's edge leaving a lip that you can stitch into. The lip does not necessarily need to surround the entire cabochon. Instead you could plan to stitch bead "ropes" up and over the cabochons surface, securely attached to the lip in several places.

Faceted Glass & Cut Crystal beads are generally geometric shapes made up of many flat surfaces or facets to catch and reflect light. They come in a wide variety of finishes, including matte, transparent, iridescent and fire-washed metallics, with iridescence like an oil slick on water.

The popular Swarvorski crystals are renowned for their clarity and sparkle. These crystals have a 32% lead content which increases their brilliance and prismatic qualities. While I wouldn't recommend crystal jewelry for younger children who might ingest them, wearing leaded crystal jewelry is not considered to be a health risk.

Cloisonné beads are made of enamel fired onto a metal background, creating a stained glass or mosaic effect. Cloisonné beads vary greatly in quality, from inexpensive samples that look like poorly done paint by numbers to exquisite works of art.

Dichroic Glass beads are created in special vacuum kilns or crucibles. Layers of vaporized metals such as titanium, silicon and magnesium crystallize on the surface of the hot glass. The metalicized surface reflects one color, while a separate, completely different color is shown when light passes through the glass.

Beaded beads can stand on their own strung as a necklace or earrings, or can make up part of a larger piece of jewelry. Either way, they are certain to draw attention.

The wooden beads commonly used for macrame, with large center holes, work especially well as the base bead, and can be painted with acrylics to match your color scheme. Ideally, the base bead should be light weight - such as wood or acrylic - so that it doesn't become too heavy.

Wooden beads are much lighter than glass or stone beads of the same size, making them especially well suited to situations where weight is of issue. While many wooden beads reflect origins in native and ethnic traditions, I've also seen sleekly modern works of art that would be at home in the most contemporary of designs.

Clay beads are much less common than glass, stone or even wooden beads in most bead stores, Similar to stone, clay beads add both physical and physiological weight to a piece.

Clockwise from top: relatively inexpensive, articulated, cloisonné fish; assorted porcelain beads; acrylic and wooden beads, some painted.

Novelty Beads and Found Objects

Looking beyond your local bead store, there's a whole world of items that could be used in your work - seashells, nuts, buttons, charms, sequins, washers, coins - the selection is endless. Look around your home, studio or garage and you'll find several likely candidates.

The only limits I acknowledge in what can be used is the item's suitability for its intended purpose - both in terms of design aesthetics and function. The object should be able to withstand its intended use (unless its failure is part of an intended message in the your design). A miniature pinecone might work in an earring, but I would hesitate to use it in a bracelet where it would be subject to more wear and abuse.

Most found objects bring a back story with them. This story should work with or enhance your design theme. The connection may be direct or tangential, but it needs to exist, at least in your own mind.

Seashells, charms, sea glass, nuts and washers, river stones, pinecones, bottle caps, coins and other found objects from the artist's collection.

Testing Beads for Suitability of Purpose

You've found the beads you want to use - they're the perfect color, shapes and sizes and it seems like you're ready to finally start stitching. But, before you start, it's always wise to consider the suitability of your selected beads for their intended purpose. Some extremely beautiful beads have sharp edges which can slice through your thread, or finishes which may fade or wear badly over time. I can say from experience that it's horribly disappointing when those lovely bugle beads you selected keep chewing their way through your beading thread, leaving frayed ends and empty gaps in their place.

It's even worse when they do this after entering some one else's collection. If you simply wish to experiment, making items for your own use, you may not care about the long-term durability of a finished piece. However, if you are making an item for sale or as a gift, this is more important.

To help reduce the chance of such disappointments, I suggest doing a few simple tests to determine whether your beads can withstand the wear they will experience as part of the finished item.

Color and Light-Fastness

Unlike artists' paints, beads do not come with light-fastness ratings. The simplest way to check for light fastness is to make two strings consisting of 3-6 beads of each variety you plan to use in a project. Put one away somewhere that you will remember it. Hang the other string in a south or west facing window and leave it there for a few weeks, using a little tab of invisible tape. Three to four weeks later, compare the sample hung in the window to the one you stored away. If any of the beads have faded noticeably you'll likely want to drop them from your project. Better yet - test beads for light-fastness as you buy them. Of note, color-lined beads seem particularly susceptible to fading.

Silver Lined Beads are a special case in that their color does not generally fade, but their silver lining often tarnishes and darkens over time. Once this happens, I don't know of a way of reversing the effect, and the difference in appearance is quite dramatic.

Testing for Sharp Edges

Because in my experience bugle beads often have sharp edges which can cut through bead thread, I highly recommend testing all bugle varieties before including them in your project. And it doesn't hurt to test other bead types as well since bugles are simply the most common suspect. Any bead with a flat, sharp looking edge close to the thread hole should be tested.

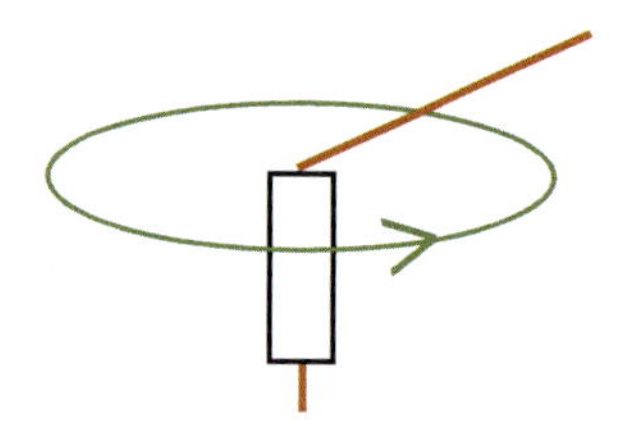

Test for sharp edges by rotating the thread at a 60° angle to bead edge. Test both ends, one at a time.

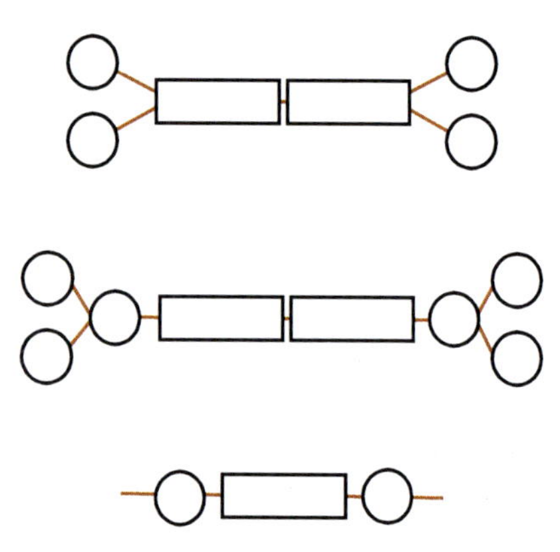

1) Danger! The angle at which the thread exits the bugle beads exposes it to additional wear if the bugles have sharp edges. 2 and 3) Safer. Alternate beads added at either end to protect beading thread.

To test for sharp edges, thread a bead onto a length of beading thread, then holding onto the bead with one hand, pull the thread taut at a sixty degree angle from the bead and rotate it a couple of times around the bead's edge. If you see signs of shredding, discard that bead and try another bugle. If the thread shows signs of shredding with your second test bead as well consider dropping those bugles from your project. Or plan to use them as accent beads where you run the thread straight through the bugles into another bead at either end, avoiding pressure against the sharp edges.

Wear & Handling Requirements

It is also worth giving some thought to how the item will be used, and how the intended usage might affect the materials you choose.

Some considerations are simple; for instance, I think that earrings generally shouldn't weigh too much. As basic as this sounds, the weight from glass and stone beads adds up quickly. If I want to use a large (read heavy) focal bead, I tend to use fewer total beads or make sure the other beads are very lightweight so that the earring is comfortable to wear.

Bracelets suffer more abuse and wear than almost any other piece of jewelry, especially during the winter months, when donning and removing heavy outerwear. If you've ever caught a bracelet or watchband in your coat sleeve, you know what I'm talking about. All of the beads and findings used in bracelet construction need to be able to handle this abuse.

If an item will be permanently attached to a garment then cleaning requirements should be considered as well. Will the beads or finishes change or suffer damage in the laundry, with dry cleaning?

Thinking about the wear, usage and cleaning requirements before you begin helps to insure the ultimate success of your project as an item of wearable art.

Findings and Closures

Selecting jewelry findings which support and compliment your work is an important and often overlooked aspect of the overall success of most jewelry projects. Findings should be functionally and aesthetically suited to their intended role in your piece, not chosen at random as an afterthought.

It is worthwhile to visit a local bead store or do some online research to see what is available; a quick glance through any online bead store presents an incredible range of findings in a dizzying array of shapes, metals and finishes. The key is determining the best findings for your particular piece.

First consider function. Earrings, for instance, obviously need a way to hang from an ear. But do you want clip-ons, posts, hoops, lever backs or earwires? The array of options is quite large; each saying something a little different about the jewelry's style and intended owner.

Besides doing its functional job, the findings must help support your design choices. Continuing with earrings, lever backs are more secure, but not quite as stylish as ear wires, while clip on earrings speak to me of old elegance and grandmother's costume jewelry. What emotions or adjectives do you use to describe your theme? Look for findings that support that.

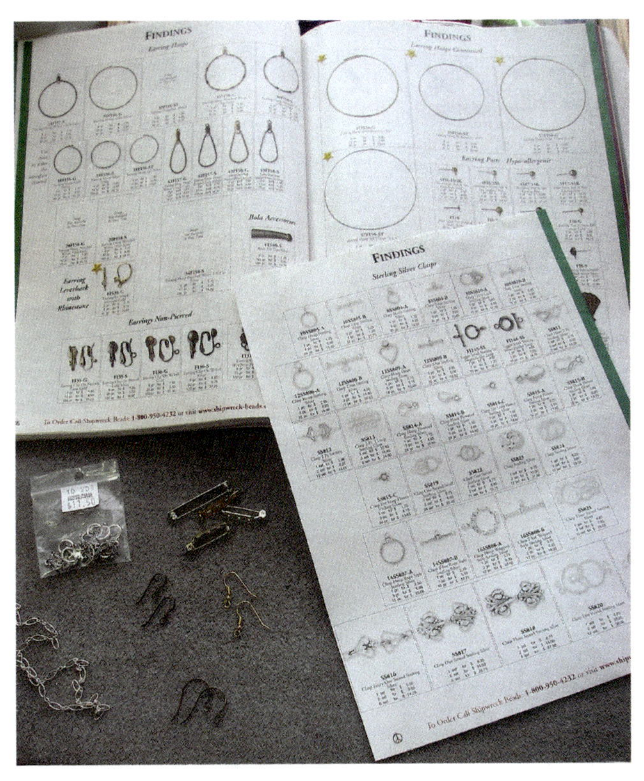

Pages from an old Shipwreck Beads' catalog, and a few findings from the artist's stash, including several styles of ear wires.

Closures

Most bracelets and many necklaces will require some form of closure. At its essence, a closure is a way of connecting two disparate parts. It should be easy to open, but secure when closed. Beyond this essential point lie questions of its aesthetic role in your design and the very practical consideration of how will you attach the closure to your piece. Ideally, the closure should be not only functional, but should be an integral part of your design.

Toggle Clasps. Composed of interlocking loop and bar components, toggle clasps are a relatively secure closure, especially when under the influence of gravity, such as in a necklace. The two components can be quite simple or ornate, the 'loop' taking a variety of closed forms. Each side has one or more anchor points where the clasp can be attached to your work.

Cord End Clasps. Most frequently used with thicker materials such as leather, satin, hemp or rubber cording, a paired cap is slipped over each cord end then crimped to anchor it securely. I use them rarely with freeform peyote, but they work well as clasps for beaded cords used to display beaded beads.

Decorative metal, glass, abalone and plastic buttons.

Two toggle clasps - note the anchor points.
Two cord end clasps, one end clamped to beaded cord.

Buttons as Closures

Buttons are some of my favorite closures, especially for bracelets! Pretty as any bead, they are visually more substantial than most traditional closures which suits my designs. A beautiful button can act as the primary accent or focus of the backside of the bracelet. A beaded loop typically completes the button closure.

Shank buttons are particularly easy to work with. The button's shank protects the bead work, reducing stress and wear at the attachment point.

Shankless buttons, or buttons with thread holes, should only be used as closures if the thread holes are recessed to protect the beading thread from wear.

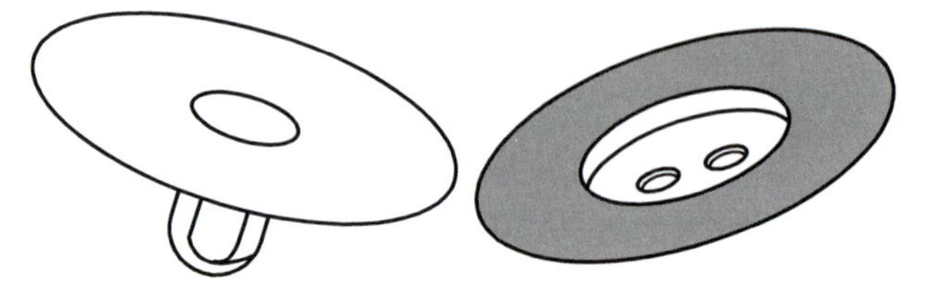

Shank button and shankless buttons. Ideally, thread holes should be recessed to protect threads from wear.

Selecting Beads for Your Project

A Recipe for Freeform Peyote

Structural Beads - ***8-12 varieties, at least 3 sizes***

2-4 varieties size 6° beads

2-4 varieties size 8°

4-7 varieties size 11° or 12°

Accent Beads

2-5 varieties hex, triangular, bugle, square, smaller pressed glass, etc.

Focal Beads

1 large, spectacular bead and/or several cool beads

Design Choices

Theme

Value

Color

Visual & Physical Texture

Size

Now that we've considered our options, it's time to finalize our selections. As you make your selections, keep in mind the need for both harmony and contrast. Choose enough bead types to give your design variation, but not so many that it looses coherence. The larger your intended project, the more bead varieties you can use; however, too many different bead types will make a small project look disjointed.

Start by looking through your personal collection before heading to the store to purchase beads for your next project. Make a sample strand of the beads you think might work by stringing three to six beads from each type onto a length of beading thread with a stop bead at either end. If a particular bead type looks poor in the test strand trust that it will look equally poor in your finished project.

If you plan to shop for additional beads, take this sample strand with you, along with a sample of your color scheme. You'll find it much easier to find the beads you need.

Playing with bead choices for a potential project.

Test strands for several different beading projects. The blue and white strands in the center are actually one doubled strand for my Ocean Waves collar.

Tools and Materials

While it's easy to spend a pretty penny on beads, the tools and materials required for freeform peyote work are relatively minimal. For a basic set up, you'll need little more than beading needles and thread, scissors and a flat surface or tray to hold your working beads.

My primary workspace in my studio with work in progress.

Threads

Silamide™ spools and cardboard bobbins, Nymo™ bobbins at left, Superlon™ at right.

Using the right thread is as important to the success of your bead project as choosing the right beads. Standard sewing thread is likely to cause trouble during stitching - tangles and breakage - and does not tend to wear well in beaded items. Instead you want a thin, strong, waxed thread made specifically for beading. I prefer that the thread also have a certain degree of stiffness, as I find this helps the bead work keep its shape over time.

Silamide™ is my long-time favorite thread for this purpose (though Superlon™ is giving it a good run for the money). A two-ply twisted nylon thread, Silamide was originally produced for the hand tailoring industry. It is strong, wear resistant, has a good weight, doesn't tangle easily and comes in a wide range of bold colors. You can find Silamide in spools and sometimes on 40yd cardboard bobbins.

Nymo™ was the only beading thread available at my local beadstore back in the early nineties when I began beading. Made of waxed nylon, Nymo comes in a range of sizes, from 00-FF. The finest, 00 would be my recommendation for freeform peyote work. I personally don't care for Nymo because it has less body than Silamide and I have a greater tendency to split stitches when using it, accidentally stitching through previous thread. Splitting stitches makes it much more difficult to adjust tensioning or reverse stitching.

Superlon™ looks similar to Nymo, but has much better manners in my opinion. A nylon, parallel fiber thread with almost no stretch (unlike Nymo), Superlon comes in a fantastic range of contemporary colors. Available in two sizes: AA - fine (my preference) and D - medium fine (slightly heavier than Nymo's size D).

All three can be found at most bead shops. Nymo is also commonly sold in many larger chain craft stores.

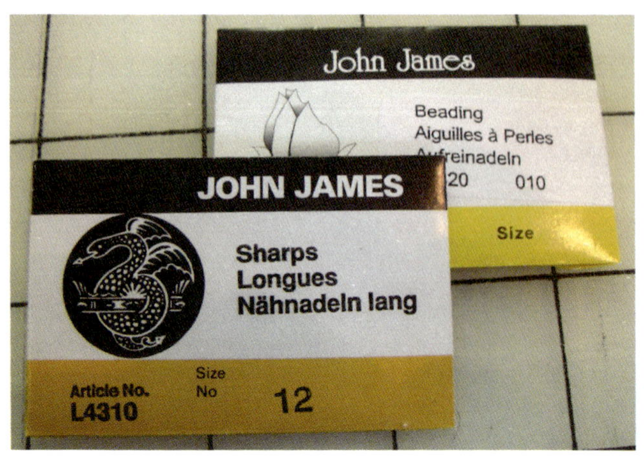

Beading needles are considerably finer than standard sewing needles.

Basic tool set, including (clockwise from top right) measuring tape, hemostat, matches, beeswax, film canister for broken needles, lighter, gelato spoon, thread cutter, embroidery scissors and pliers.

Needles

Beading needles are finer than other needles, with extremely small eyes designed to make it easier to fit multiple thread passes through a size 11° bead hole. Standard beading needles are quite long and are designed for loom work. Because we will be dealing with lots of tight angles, I prefer to work with a shorter needle. My favorites are size 12 sharps by John James™.

Place the occasional broken needle in a designated 'sharps' container - old film canisters work well.

Scissors and Thread Cutters

It's worth buying a pair of small, sharp embroidery scissors. Their fine tips allow you to snip the threads close to your bead work, minimizing thread tails. They can also get in between beads if the worst occurs and you need to cut out a thread tangle. I am particularly fond of my 4" curved embroidery scissors by Gingher™.

When traveling by plane, pack your scissors in your checked luggage or leave them at home. Since security guidelines change so frequently, I now pack a pendant thread cutter made by Clover™ instead. I have never had a problem including it in my carryon on a domestic flight. But always check airport security regulations before you travel as they can and do change.

Pliers and Hemostats

As you work, you may find that it becomes difficult to pull the needle through some beads due to the number of previous thread passes. You can use a pair of flat-nosed pliers or hemostats to help pull the needle through these beads. But be careful.

If the bead hole is too full, you can break the bead if you force the needle through; this leaves an ugly gap that must be covered over and can damage the beading thread as well. If a bead hole feels tight, I'll use the pliers. If it feels impassable, then I choose a different route for my thread, either through other beads, or by creating a bridge over the tight beads. This will make more sense as you go.

Two sizes of Vellus™, porcelain watercolor palette and metal beading trays.

Bead trays and cloths

You will need something to hold your beads as you work. While I've tried a number of paint dishes, trays and lids, I now use a beading cloth made from Vellux™ almost exclusively.

Beads sit on the surface of the Vellux™ and do not roll around. I pour little mounds of the various beads that I think I'll use. The cloth seems to hold the beads poised for use, making it very easy to pick them up with my beading needle.

When it's time to clean up, it's easy to scoop the beads back into their containers (I use a gelato tasting spoon for this purpose). Last I checked, you won't find these cloths at most bead stores. My beading cloth came from a friend who bought a blanket and cut it up, but you can also find Vellux at some fabric stores. When I work on the couch or in the car, I put my beading cloth into a wooden tray so that I have a flat,

Lighting

Make sure that your workspace has good lighting to help avoid eyestrain. Not surprisingly, bright, indirect natural light is the best. The next best option is true-color task lighting.

Because color is so important to the success of any bead work, I highly recommend selecting your beads using natural or true-color light. I don't recommend selecting beads under standard incandescent or fluorescent lighting unless you know for a fact that your work will only ever be seen under that light source.

I have three task lights that I use regularly; two folding portable OTT-LITES™ which I can take to workshops and a larger floor lamp. If you had to select only one light, I'd recommend a portable desktop version as they're more versatile. I recently discovered that OTT now makes a battery powered version of my folding lights - quite tempting for beading on the go, such as at workshops.

Portable, desk-top Ott-Lite™, top folds down to turn off.

Bead Storage Containers

I do not have a tried and true bead storage system. I've gone through several different organizational methods, and at this point, my beads are sorted into two main categories: structural beads and accent/focal beads, then by color. I store most of my beads in plastic drawers and boxes. Some beads come in tubes or other reusable containers which I simply sort into my current stash. If the beads don't come in reclosable containers, I immediately transfer them into one of my favorite storage options:

Tic Tac™ boxes. If you or someone you know eats a lot of Tic Tacs, you might consider asking them to save the boxes as they make great bead storage containers. Alternatively, Seattle-based Fusion Beads (*see Resources*) sells empty flip-top lid, plastic boxes in several sizes. The largest size (4" x 1.5" x .5") holds an entire hank of seed beads while the smallest size (1" x 1" x .5") is great for storing beads on the go.

Plastic Reclosable Baggies are the most space efficient storage method for individual bead lots that I have found. My favorite sizes are 3"x4" and 2"x3" for this purpose. You can find these near the beading section of most craft stores. A 3"x4" baggy will hold an entire hank of beads.

Reclosable baggies are also great for sorting and storing the beads you're using on your current project. I use the smaller 2" x 2" size for this

Top shelf of my bead storage.

purpose These baggies hold more than enough of each type of bead for most projects, and minimize the carrying size and weight when traveling.

Watchmakers' cases have to be one the prettiest ways to store a collection of beads. Originally intended to store gems, watch movements and jeweler's findings, they are small, round, glass-topped aluminum containers. They come in a variety of sizes, from about one to three inches in diameter. Though they can be hard to find, I have seen them offered a number of places recently. I've seen the larger size at several kitchen or bed and bath stores, sold as spice containers. Lee Valley Tools (*see Resources*), on the Internet, offers several different sets, nicely packaged in neat cardboard or metal boxes.

While I love the look of these containers, they seem more suitable for long term bead storage than for travel to me. But they are so pretty, they are well worth consideration.

Beading on the Go

My to go box packed with supplies for several small beading projects, including rings and beaded beads.

I do a lot of my beading away from home and have developed a very compact bead kit that easily fits into a backpack, purse or even a large pocket. Everything I need for one large project (such as a necklace) or several smaller projects (bracelets or smaller) fits into the box except for my larger beading cloth, which I wrap around the box as padding.

If I can't close the box, I've packed too many beads and simply pare down until it all fits. Paring down includes making sure I don't have too many types of beads (which can also result in a disjointed project), or too many beads of a particular type. Excess beads go back into their primary storage containers and I'm ready to go.

Basic Kit

Soft plastic storage box

Beads in baggies or plastic boxes

Pendant thread cutter

2 Beading needles stuck in a small square of felt

Beading thread in appropriate colors

Small spoon or bead scoop (for cleanup)

Beading cloth

Optional: Pliers

Beeswax for waxing thread

Embroidery scissors

The closed box measures 4 x 6 x 1.5".

The Stitches

Freeform peyote is an organic blend of a number of different stitching and beading techniques. Each project is a unique mixture of these stitches along with a heavy does of creative license. Before jumping into a freeform peyote project, it helps to have a fair handle on the basics. If you've never worked with the peyote stitch before, I'd suggest stitching up a small sample of even-count flat peyote before you start in on a larger project. Once you have five to six lines of stitching under your belt and are comfortable with the basic stitch pattern, you'll be ready to move on to more freeform work.

Getting Started

I use a single strand of beading thread for most of my freeform peyote. While a doubled strand may provide an extra sense of security, I find that the additional bulk is a poor trade-off, especially after having broken beads trying to wedge one more pass of the needle through a packed bead hole. In the course of the stitching you will stitch through each bead multiple times. My experience indicates that this provides more protection in the event of thread breakage than a doubled thread.

Measure out 3 to 4 feet of beading thread, a bit longer than you would generally use in hand stitching. The length is a compromise between ease of work and minimizing thread starts and stops. Changing threads slows your work and adds to the bulk of thread in your bead holes, but thread that's too long develops a mind of its own, twisting and tangling at the least provocation.

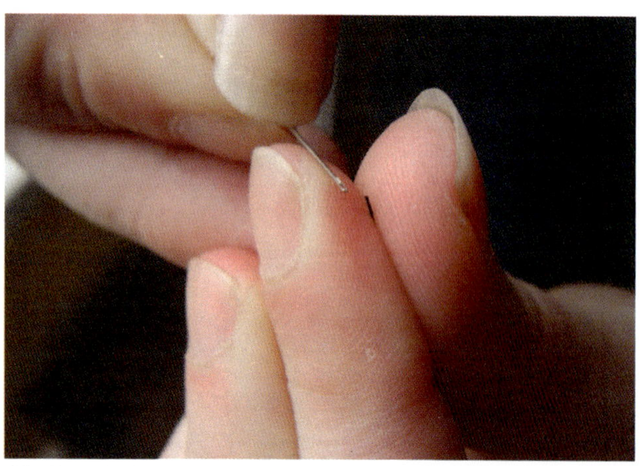

To thread the needle, pinch the thread between the thumb and forefinger of your non-dominant hand and bring the eye of the needle to it. Photo credit JFH.

Threading the Needle

The eyes of beading needles are quite small, which can make them more difficult to thread. Depending upon your choice of needle and thread, you may be able to use a needle threader, but I wouldn't count on it.

Instead, try holding the thread pinched between the thumb and forefinger of your non-dominant hand so that only the tip of the thread is visible. The thread tip will look like a tiny splinter peaking from between your thumb and finger. The thread is now quite stable. Holding the needle in your dominant hand, bring it to the thread and carefully place the eye of the needle over the 'splinter'. This is the method I learned to use before my eye surgeries, when I couldn't really see the eye of the needle to thread it, so I know it works.

Position the needle five to eight inches from one thread end. You shouldn't need and don't want a terribly long thread tail. Often the eye of the needle will damage your stitching thread as you work. When this happens the entire tail should be considered waste and you shouldn't reposition your needle to use the tail. You don't want the damaged thread to become part of your work.

Previous page: detail of "Autumn Glory" bracelet.

Thinking about Thread Color

When I began beading, my local beadstore had two color choices for beading thread - black and white. Some intrepid beaders I knew used markers to color their beading thread, with varying degrees of success. Unsatisfied with that option, I convinced myself it simply important to match values.

As colored beading threads became available - first Sylamide, then others, I happily matched both the color and value of my beading thread to my projects. My goal was that the thread blend seamlessly so that it would be invisible in the finished product.

A couple of years ago, I had the good fortune to take an advanced workshop with David Chatt. Under his tutelage I began to explore the subtleties of color that the beading thread can bring to a piece, seen through transparent and semi-transparent beads.

The single line of beads above shows the three bead colors used in the peyote stitch sample below. Creative use of colored threads increases the color range.

Adding a Stop Bead

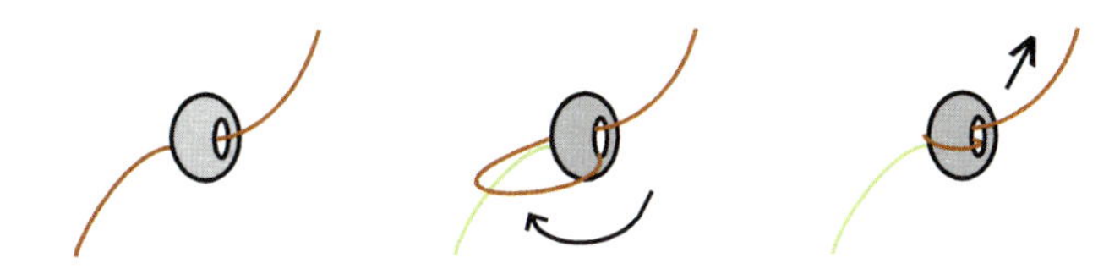

Start each project with a stop bead. The stop bead helps hold everything in place in the early stages of work. You can plan to include the stop bead in the final piece, or to remove it once the first few rows of stitching are complete. If you plan to remove the stop bead, use a contrasting color as a reminder so that you don't accidentally include it in your stitching. If the stop bead will remain, include it in your initial bead count.

String the stop bead onto your thread, pulling it through until a six inch tail remains. Run your needle through the bead again in the same direction as before so that it forms a loop around the bead. Pull the thread snug around the bead, making sure to maintain the thread tail. You will work the tail into your piece in a little while.

What to do with the Stop Bead. Once you have completed several rows of peyote stitch you can remove the stop bead or incorporate it into your work. Either way, remove the thread loop around the stop bead by slipping your needle under the loop and pulling it loose. Remove the bead or not based upon your design. Thread the tail onto a beading needle and stitch through several inches of beading, as you would when changing threads (*See next section*).

Changing Threads

Change threads when you have five to seven inches remaining between your needle and your work (do not count the thread tail). Finish off the thread end by stitching back through your work in a zigzagging pattern. Change directions at least twice including at least one full u-turn, backtracking through a previous bead. You can make a direction change as often as every third or fourth bead. Three to four directions changes, including at least one u-turn, is usually sufficient.

Finishing Thread Ends. As you stitch, periodically test the last bead you added. At first the bead will pull loose quite easily; retighten the tension and keep stitching. With each direction change, the bead will feel more secure. After several direction changes, and the last bead feels quite secure, clip the thread tail close to your bead work.

Start a new thread the same way you finish old ones; run your needle through at least 3 inches of existing beads, backtracking and changing directions at least twice. I leave a 3" thread tail so that I can check tensioning as I stitch. With each direction change I tug on the thread; if the thread tail shortens keep stitching. When the thread feels quite secure you can clip the tail and begin adding new beads.

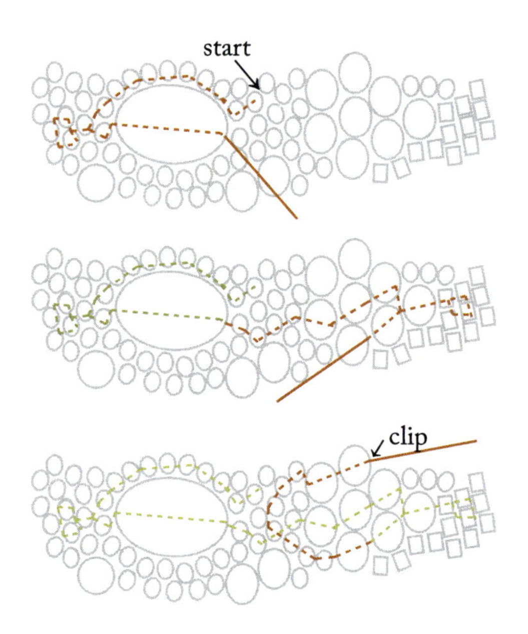

Knots. I do not use knots in my work. They are difficult to stitch around and have a tendency to come undone. If you finish off the ends as suggested above, then knots aren't necessary.

However, if you still prefer to knot your ends, feel free to use them. To make a knot, come up between two beads and circle your needle around a single thread. Pull your thread most of the way through, leaving a small loop. Run your needle through the thread loop and pull it taut. Clip your thread close to the work. But remember that by itself, a knot is not as secure as running your thread through several inches of stitching.

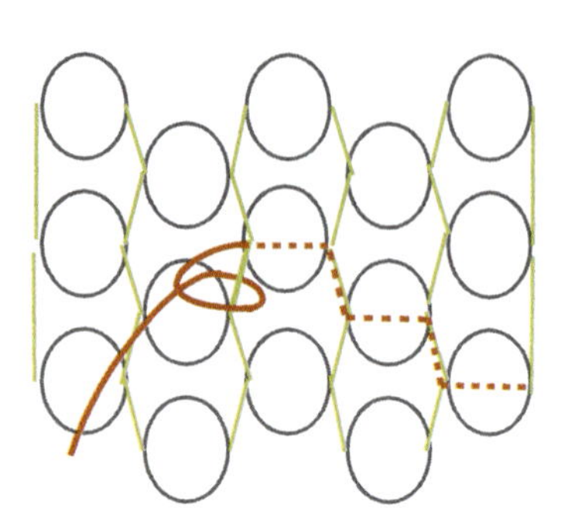

Above right: Finishing off a thread end with two u-turns and several direction changes. Clip thread close to beading.
Right: Tieing a simple knot.

Basic Peyote Stitches

Even-Count Flat Peyote

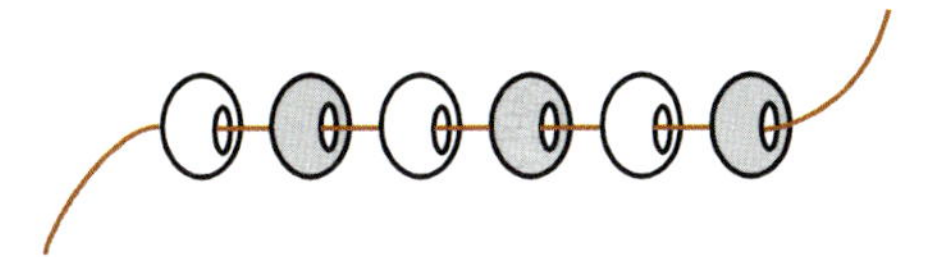

String an even number of beads. Even-numbered beads (row one) are shaded grey.

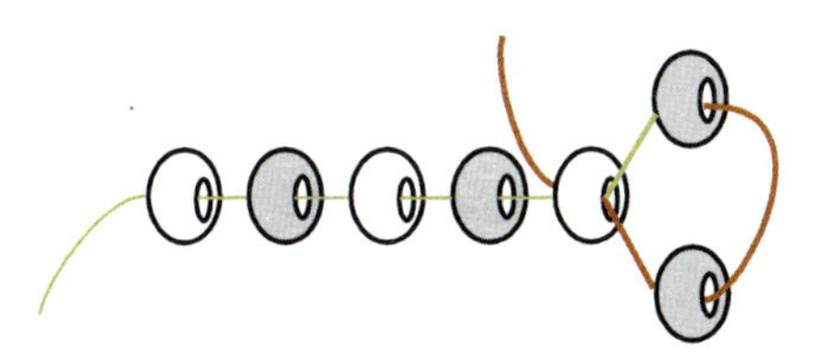

Starting Row Three. Add the first bead of row three, then reverse stitching directions, going back through the second to last bead. The two beads should sit on top of each other.

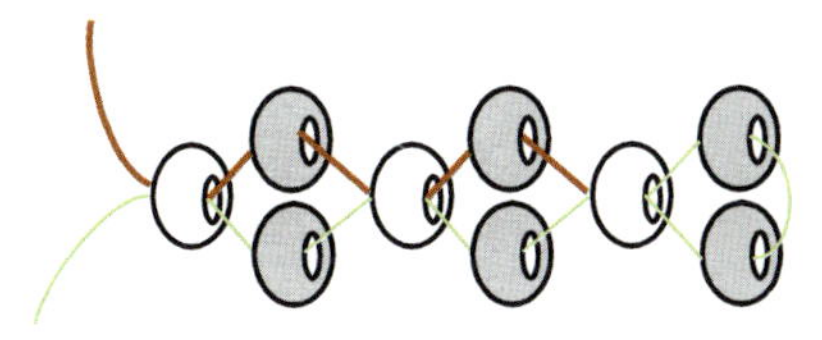

Continue adding beads and stitching through every other bead until the end of the row.

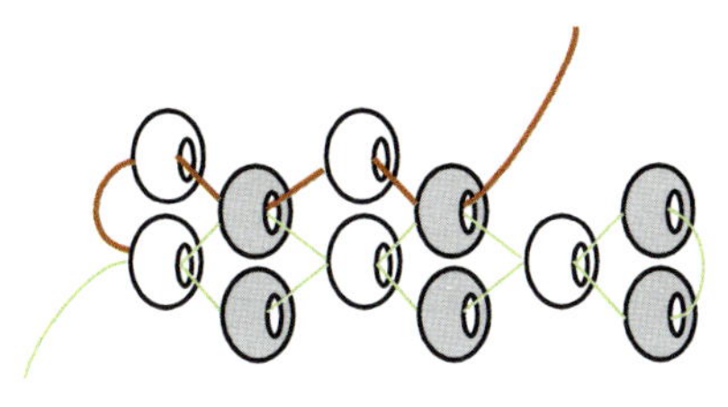

Starting Row Four. Add a bead, then stitch back through the last bead of row three. Continue adding a bead, skipping a bead, stitching through every other bead, until the end of the row. Reverse stitching directions and continue for each row.

String an even number of beads onto your beading thread. These beads will form your first and second row of stitches, which will make sense when you start on row three. The even-numbered beads are row one and the odd-numbered beads form row two. In my diagrams the even-numbered beads (Row One) are shaded to help distinguish the rows. Remember to count your stop bead if it will be part of your finished work.

To start Row Three - the first real row of peyote stitch - thread a single bead onto your needle. Reverse your stitching direction and skip over the last bead in row one, stitching through the last odd-numbered bead. Pull the thread taut so that the new bead sits just above the last bead in row one. At this stage, I think it looks sort of like two insect eyes on a dragonfly body.

String another bead and skip the even-numbered bead, stitching through the next odd bead. Continue adding a bead, skipping a bead, stitching through every other bead until you reach the end of the row. Keep your thread tension tight and consistent as you work.

Row Four. Now you're ready to double back and start row four. String another bead, then stitch back through the last bead in row three. Continue adding a bead, stitching through every other bead. Reverse the stitching direction at the end of each row.

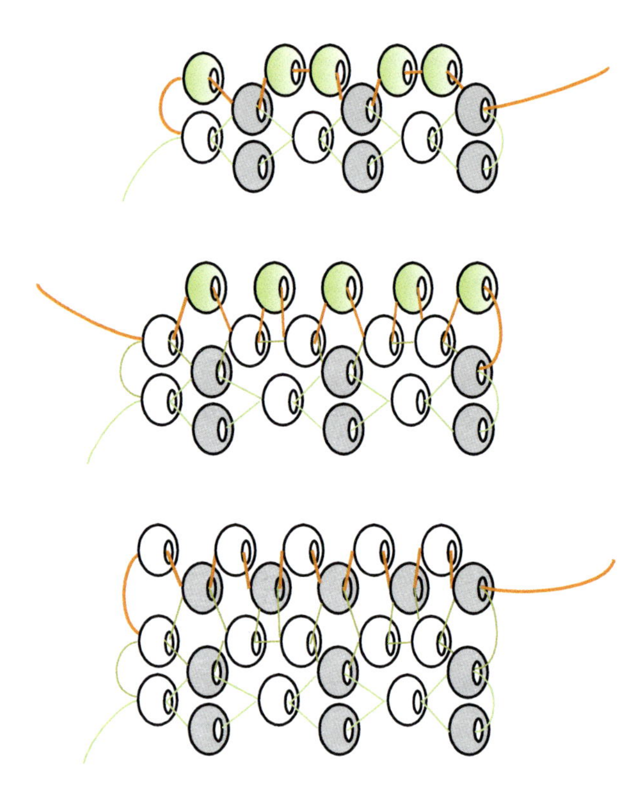

Increase worked over two rows. First row - two beads added in place of one. Second row, beads are added between each bead of the row before. This sample starts with three beads, and finishes with five beads per row. Work subsequent rows as normal.

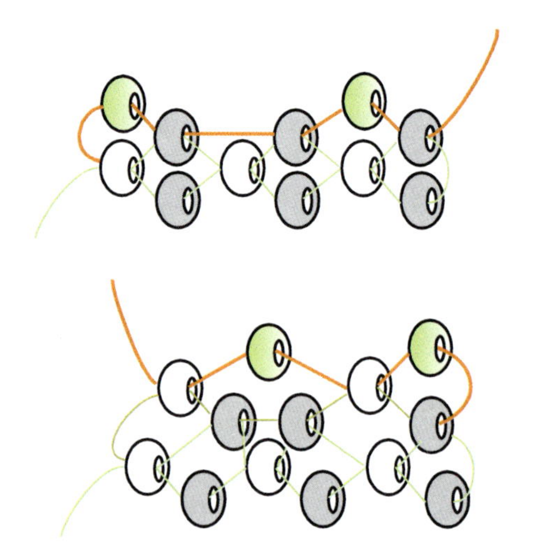

Decrease worked over two rows. First row - do not add a bead, but stitch through two beads of base. Second row - put one bead in the gap and pull the tension taut to take up the slack.

Increases and Decreases

Sometimes it is necessary to add or remove beads from the standard peyote stitch, especially when you are working beads of different shapes and sizes. These additions and deletions, along with steady tension, help prevent the appearance of thread gaps which would detract from the overall appearance of your piece. Increases may cause your work to bulge or buckle to accommodate the new beads. You can use this tendency to create additional texture, or you can work to minimize the buckling through careful control of the thread tensions in the transition. Both increases and decreases are worked over two rows.

Increases. In the first row, add two beads in a single stitch instead of one. The next row, add an extra bead between each pair of beads to set the new width. The extra beads squashed between the increase beads will protest and tend to stick out - keep your tension taught and subsequent rows will fix the problem. Continue stitching as normal unless your work requires additional increases.

Decreases. Omit adding a bead and stitch through two beads of the previous row. The thread will seem to gape like an empty tooth socket; pull it snug across the gap taking up as much slack as possible. Subsequent rows will fill the gap and make it look better.

In the next row, add only one bead where the two had been. Then continue stitching as normal.

Two-Drop Peyote

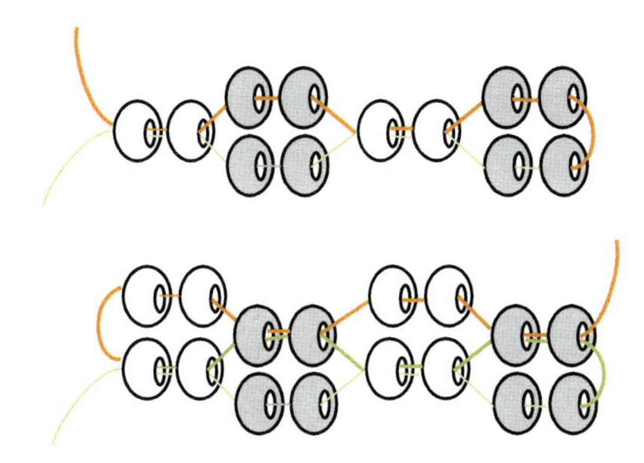

In this variation, treat pairs of beads as individual units. Instead of adding one, skipping one, stitching through one, you will add two, skip two and stitch through two beads of the previous row with each stitch.

Circular Peyote - Stitching in the Round

Circular peyote is particularly useful for creating rings, beaded cords, tubes and loop beads.

String a loop of beads, circling through the loop at least twice. Coming up out of the loop, pick up a bead and begin peyote stitch - skipping one bead in the loop and stitching through the next. Continue around the loop.

If you strung an even number of beads originally, you will finish the row by stitching through the original loop bead, then your first addition. You are set to start the next row. At the end of each row, you will stitch through two beads - the last bead of the bottom row and the first bead of the row you just completed.

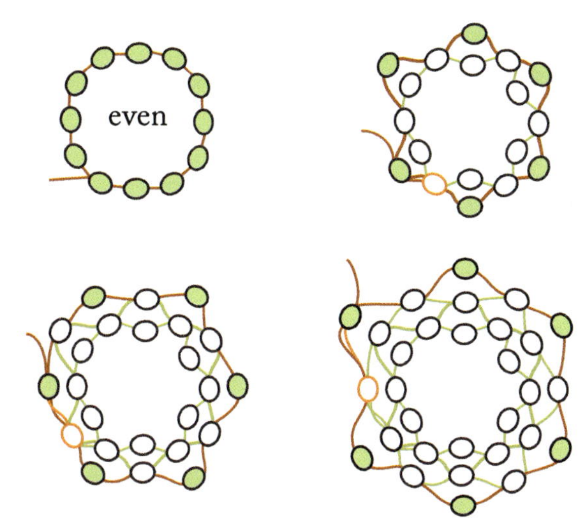

Even count circular peyote stitch - the starting bead (orange outline) shifts one clockwise with each new row.

If you strung an odd number of beads, finish the row by stitching through the first bead of the row you just completed. It looks a bit lopsided, but you don't have to watch for the step up.

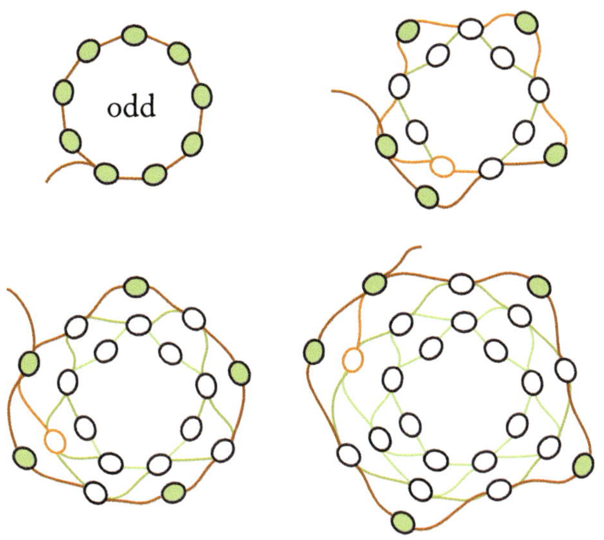

Odd count circular peyote stitch - at the end of each tow you pass through the first bead added to that row.

Freeform Peyote

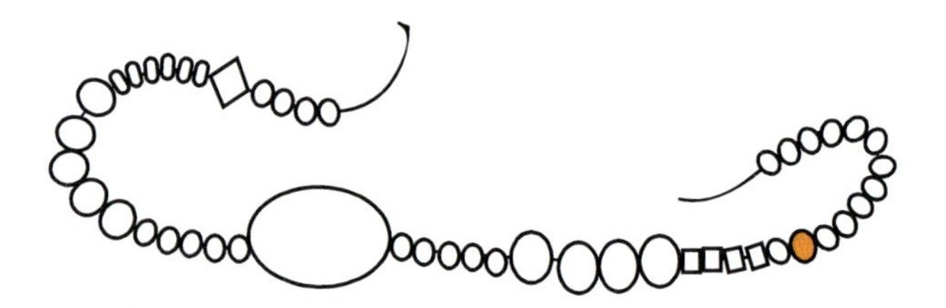

Starting Lengths

Start with a stop bead. Then string groups of your structural beads, interspersed with a few accent beads, until you are just shy of the intended length of your project. Refer back to *Chapter Two - Measuring Your Subject* for additional assistance.

String at least 5/8" to 1 1/2" worth of each structural bead selection before changing types. This will help establish your initial blocks of color. Don't mix colors or types of beads within the blocks; remember you're going for organic, not random.

You will work freeform peyote above and below this starting line.

Earrings. The stop bead marks the bottom of your earring. String beads the length of the earring, minus any fringe you plan to add. When you reach the top of the earring, string sufficient beads to loop around the finding (*see Adding a Closure Loop*); size 15° beads can work well for this loop.

Rings. I find it easiest to work rings in the round using circular peyote. The initial ring should be a loose fit, as some of the slack will be taken up in the stitching; how much depends upon the techniques you decide to use.

Bracelets or Cuffs. String sufficient beads to fit comfortably around the wrist adding in the overlap for your closure if necessary. If you want to string your focal bead immediately, make sure to place it somewhere in the middle half of the length, like a watch face, so that it will be visible when worn.

Necklaces and Collars. I find it easier to work larger pieces in sections. This gives me more control over the shape of the finished piece. I often start with the center front and work my way around to the back of the neck.

Assuming you will work your piece in sections, decide whether you wish to work the center section from side to side or from top to bottom. Working from side to side will most closely resemble working on a bracelet. If you plan to work from side to side, string beads equal to the full width of the center section. Otherwise, string beads equal to the height of your center.

If you made a paper mock-up of your necklace shape, use it to help guide your stitching.

Adding a Closure Loop

You may find it easier to create the loop if the last bead of the main body, the turn bead, differs from the beads before it or inside the loop. Because the turn bead is a thread bottleneck, it can help to use a bead that has a larger thread hole.

Size 8° or smaller seed beads work especially well for the loop as they will fit more easily around your button or closure without adding too much bulk to the closure area. String enough beads so that the loop strand fits around your closure when folded in half with a little room to spare. Once the loop is long enough, run your needle back through the turn bead.

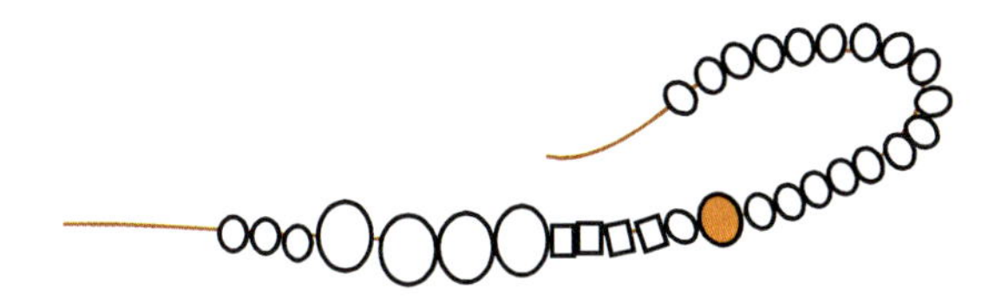

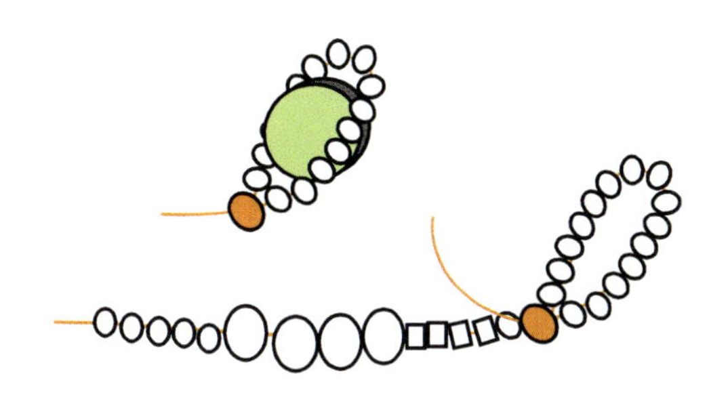

String beads for the loop closure, testing to make sure the closure fits through it easily with some slack – the loop will shrink with stitching.

Continuing to stitch

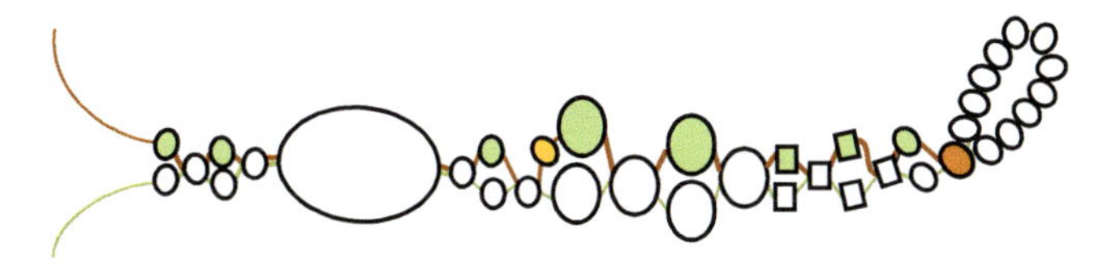

Starting the first real row of peyote stitch (shaded green). Note the orange turn bead for the loop and the yellow transition bead filling the potential thread gap between bead sizes. No attempt is made to go around the accent bead.

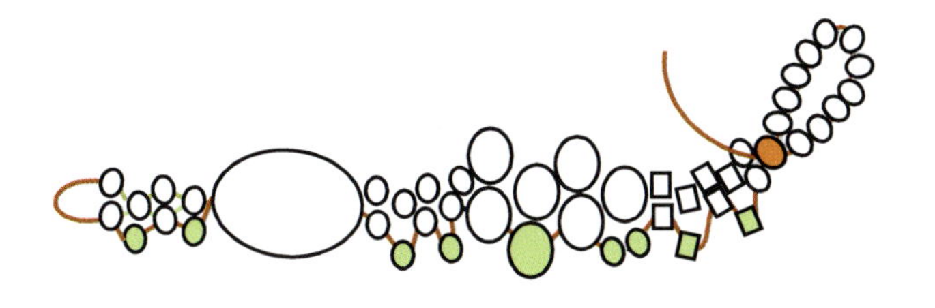

Working the fourth row in a clockwise fashion below the original center line. Needles passes through the larger accent bead in this row, too. Hold off starting peyote stitch on the loop until next pass.

Now you're ready to start the peyote stitch. For this first pass, match the new beads to the beads in each section.

When changing bead sizes between sections, such as going from a size 11° to a size 6° (or vice versa) you may need to add an extra, smaller transition bead or two to hide the beading thread. These extra beads will help merge the two sections visually. Complete at least 3-4 rows of stitching before moving colors more aggressively.

Don't try to stitch around any particularly large beads at this point. Go through its bead hole instead and pick up the peyote stitch again on the other side. Do this for several rows until the peyote stitch widens enough to consider running a bridge around the bead.

In traditional peyote, additional rows are worked in a zigzag fashion, the new stitches building from the original line of stitching in one direction, rather like adding bricks to a wall.

For freeform peyote, I prefer to add additional rows in a clockwise fashion, circling around the original line of beading. Stitching in a circular fashion, your original line of beading becomes roughly the mid-line of the finished project. This gives you more control of the finished look of both edges and a strong center line.

Above: just finishing the third row of peyote stitch.
Below: after several additional rows of stitching. Starting to move colors and add decorative work.

Moving Textures and Colors

Once you have completed four or five rows you can start moving and adding colors and bead types. Start moving some sections into their neighbors by changing bead types before or after your original transition points. Introduce one or two completely new sections using new colors or bead types. If you decided upon color proportions before you started, keep these in mind as you work.

A transition can be subtle, taking place over the course of several rows, or it may be quite abrupt as one bead type overruns another in the space of one to two rows. Watch the edges where colors and bead types meet; the transitions should appear organic, not like bricks lined up in a wall. Bridges can also be added later to continue blending and moving colors.

At this point, you don't need to work the full length with every pass. I often find it easier to build the design by focusing on a two-to-three inch section at a time, working it for several rows, then moving on to work on its neighbors.

Decorative Techniques

Popcorn Beads

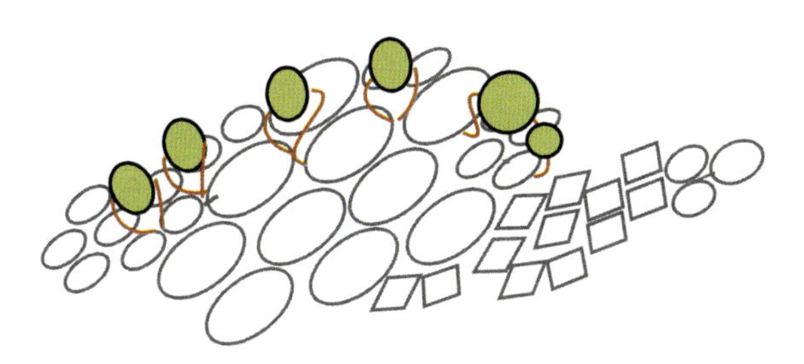

Popcorn beads worked across the surface.

In my lexicon, "popcorn" beads are individual beads added to the surface of the peyote stitch. They have a distinctly different appearance than bridges. Bridges form lines and represent movement while popcorn beads literally "pop" into existence and disappear back into the weave. Think of them as exclamation points.

If the popcorn bead is small, you can add it "between" beads – come out of one bead, add the popcorn bead, then go through the next bead in the peyote stitch base. If the popcorn bead is larger you will likely need to skip one or more beads in the base to minimize the appearance of extra beading thread. Add popcorn beads after you have completed the majority of the regular stitching.

Right: Adding a twist.
1 - Select the end points and angle of the twist. The transition length is the distance between the two end points.
2 - Right edge flipped upwards 180° to create twist.
3 - Peyote stitch worked along new top edge to secure twist.

Twists

During the first few rows of stitching it can be a bit tricky to keep the two edges distinct. In general, you will want to take some care not to confuse the two sides or your work can get a bit lumpy. However, you may choose to purposely incorporate twists as a design element.

To add a twist, flip one end over at an angle across the width. Make the twist short and tight or longer and more gradual by adjusting the end points and transition length. To hold the twist, work peyote stitch along one edge as close as you can to the ridge. Use a bridge to connect the two edges and continue stitching.

Twists will appear as a crested wave line running from one edge to the other. The wider the piece is (the more rows you've completed) when you do the twist, the taller the wave crest.

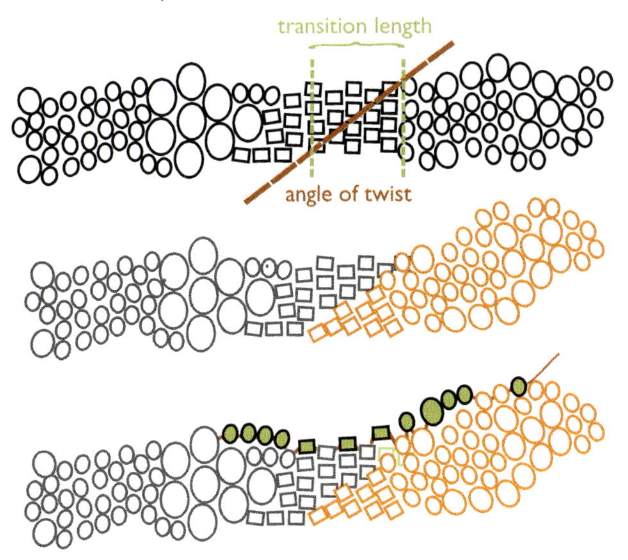

Bridges

Bridges are spans of five or more beads worked above, around or beside the regular peyote stitch. As simple as they seem, bridges are extremely versatile construction and design tools. You can use them to solve problems, work around elements and to add textural interest.

Encircling Beads. You can use bridges to go around larger beads. Once the width of the peyote stitch is close to the width of the larger bead, work a bridge to either or both of its sides.

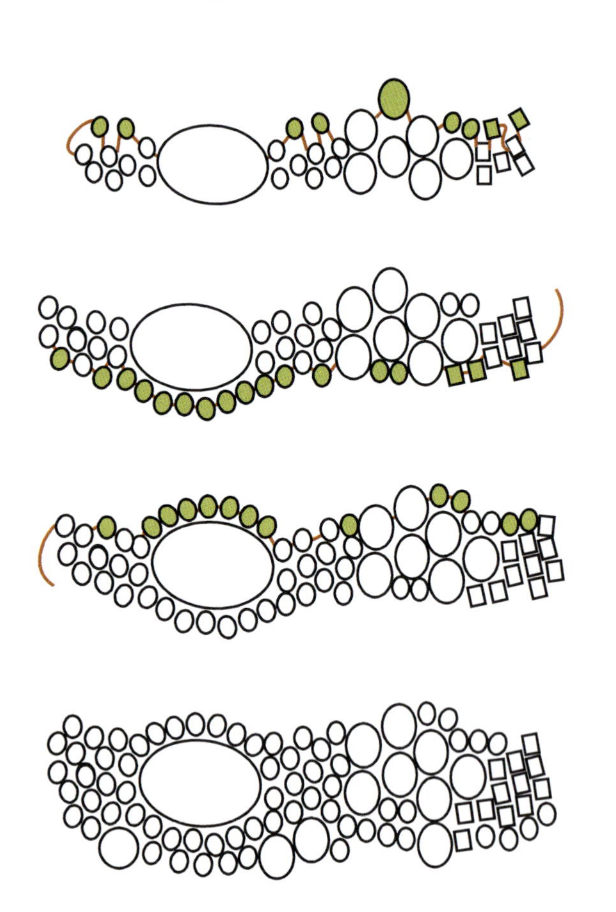

Adding bridges to either side of accent bead. Bottom: beginning to work peyote stitch off the lower bridge. Again note how we're starting to move bead sizes and shapes.

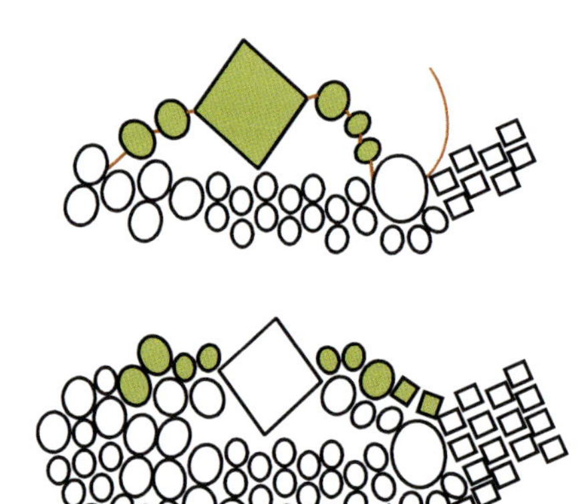

Adding an accent bead using a bridge.
Top: the smaller beads help hide excess beading thread.
Bottom: several rows of peyote stitch begin to tie the accent bead into the main body of work. Note how we are moving bead types and sizes.

Adding Accent Beads. Use bridges to add accent or focal beads. String one or more structural beads on either side of the larger bead to ease the transition. You may decide to work additional rows of peyote stitch along the bridge. The bridge will then become an alternate pathway and part of the main body of your piece.

Close up showcases several types of bridges.

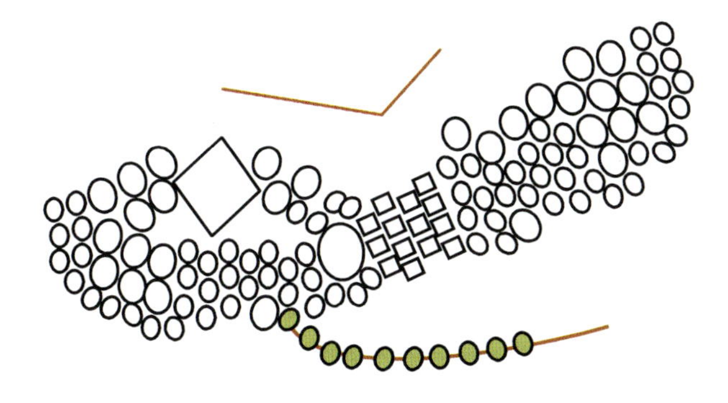

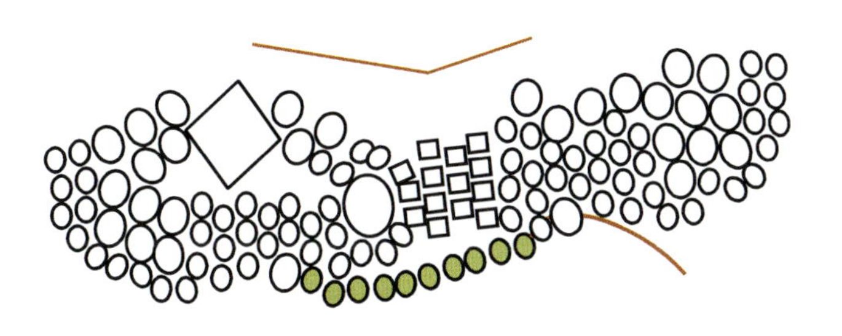

Adding a course correction bridge to straighten the upward curve. Tightening the tension straightens the curve, but may cause the main body to pucker or bulge.

Course Corrections. As you continue to stitch, your work will likely begin to curve. To straighten a curve, add a bridge on the opposite edge from the direction of the curve. The bridge should be slightly shorter than the length it needs to span. As you tighten the tension, the work will pull back towards the bridge, away from the original curve. The shorter you make a particular bridge compared to the distance it needs to span, the greater the resultant curve.

Course corrections often cause a raised ridge near your bridge. Think of the raised area as surface texture and incorporate it into your developing design. I often add a larger accent bead to course correction bridges. The raised bead work caused by the course correction will cup around the accent bead like a cuff.

Cross Bridges. Work bridges across the top of your piece to marry color sections and add visual and dimensional accents. Generally, you will not want to work additional rows of peyote stitch off of these bridges. However, you can wind and intertwine multiple bridge lines across the top of a piece to great effect.

When you create a bridge, make sure to run your needle and thread through it at least twice. This will help protect the integrity of the piece in the event of any future thread breakage.

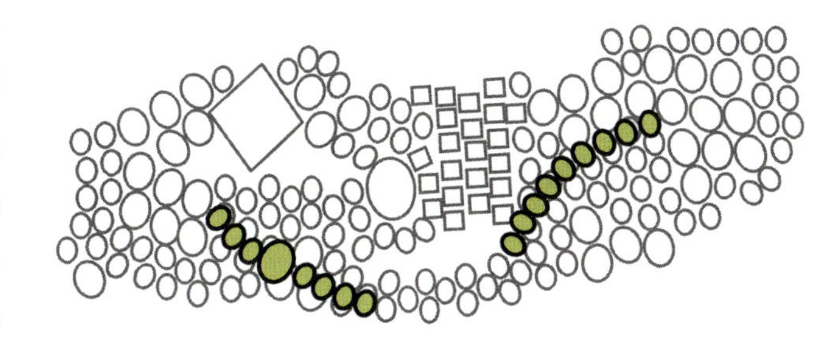

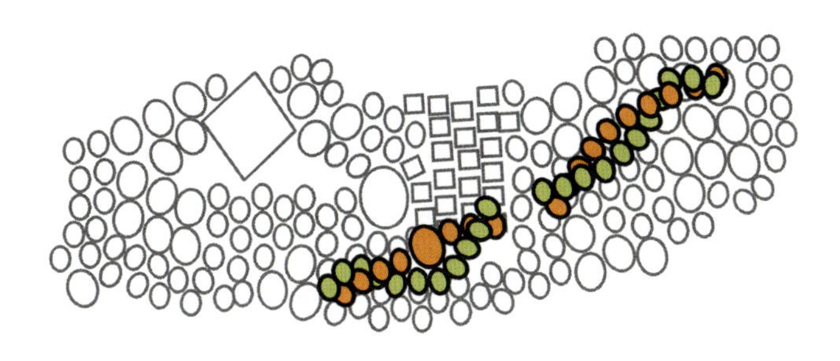

Bridges worked across the surface of the piece. Cross bridges can also interconnect or entwine.

Curves, Ruffles and Loops

At times, you will need or want to stitch along a curve, perhaps to circle a focal bead, or simply to add sinuous lines to your work. As you work around the curve, the spaces between your beading will gape along the outer, convex edge and shrink along the inner, concave side. How you deal with these variations will dramatically affect the look of your finished piece.

If you wish your beading to lay relatively flat along the horizontal plane, you will need to accommodate these changes by varying the bead sizes or adding increases and decreases to match. I generally find it easier to work along the outer, convex edge where I can focus on increases.

This pair of earrings contains excellent examples of both a single and an s-curve with larger beads used for the increases.

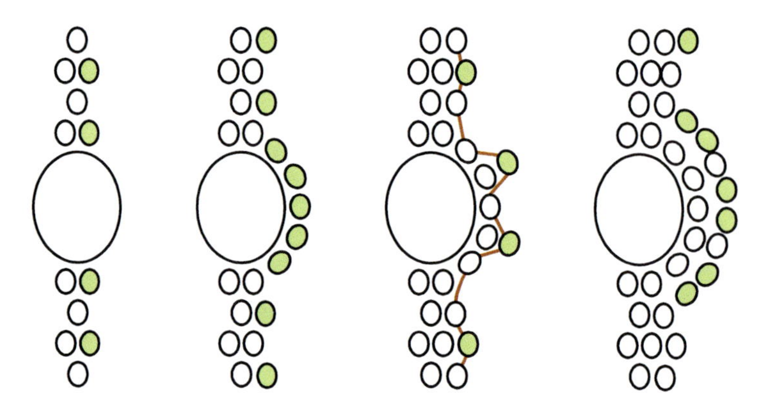

Stitching around a larger bead where the intention is to keep the bead work relatively flat and smooth - adding increases as necessary.

Working along the Convex Edge

Start by stringing a bridge that fits comfortably along the curve you wish to create. Stitch a row of regular peyote stitch, matching the bridge beads in this row (don't change bead types or sizes yet).

In the next row, add increases or larger beads as necessary to fit the larger gaps along the outer edge of the curve. It's not quite as simple as the diagram. When stitching, you'll need to judge whether each increase is necessary to fill the space. You want to keep gaps and visible thread to a minimum. The gaps will almost certainly differ in size around the curve; the variations in bead width of Czech and some Japanese seed beads can make it easier to accommodate the varying sizes.

Where the curve juts out from the main body of the work there may be pinch points where it is necessary to skip beads to keep everything laying flat, depending upon the beads you've chosen and your stitching.

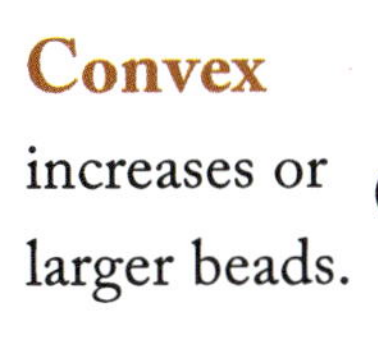

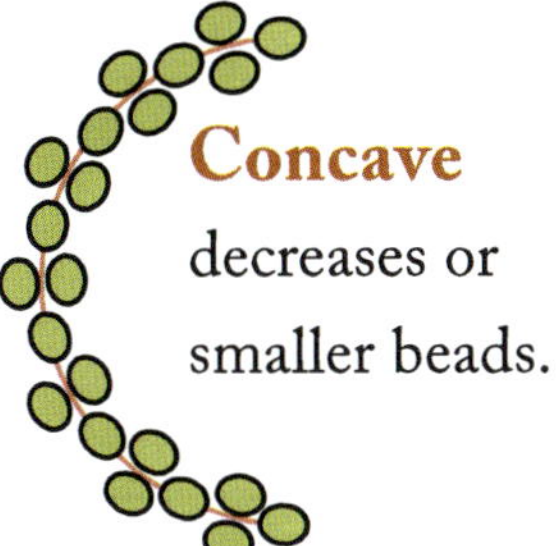

Convex increases or larger beads.

Concave decreases or smaller beads.

Walls. If you work along the curve without increases or decreases, your stitching will form a vertical wall similar to circular peyote. You could use this to create a sleeve or bezel to surround a particular bead.

Ruffles. If you add more increases than the curve requires, your beading will start to ripple or ruffle as the beading flexes to accommodate the additions. The more beads, the more pronounced the ruffle will be.

Physical Effects of Increases along a Curve

Increases	Effect
None	Wall, Collar Sleeve Bezel, Cuff
Perfect Fit	Flat curve
Extra	Ruffles, Ripples

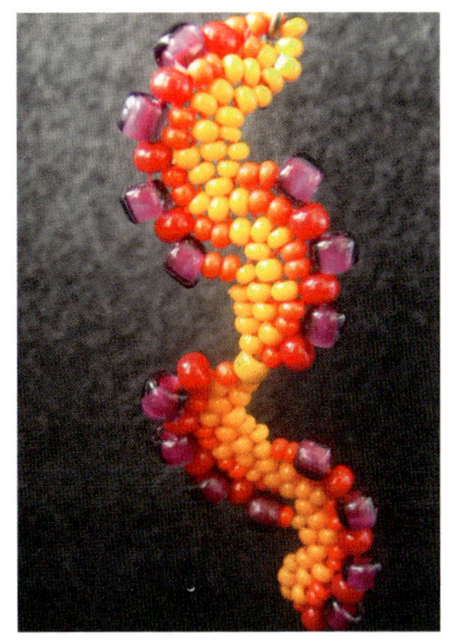

In the left hand sample, the work remains relatively flat. The ruffled sample to the right is the result of the exuberant use of increases and larger beads, as well as twists to accent the ruffles.

The bead loop on the left is from one of my early projects - it will not lay flat, and is difficult to button. Compare it to the nice, flat bead loop at right.

Loops. Most of the loops I use are more tear-drop shaped than round. As such, the increases need to be worked sensitively to maintain the shape of the loop's center. Concentrate increases primarily around the curved end with only occasional increases along the two legs.

Fringe Techniques

Hold off adding fringe until the main body of your work nears completion as it is difficult to work around and tends to get tangled in your beading thread. Also, it is easier to figure out optimum fringe placement when you have more to work with.

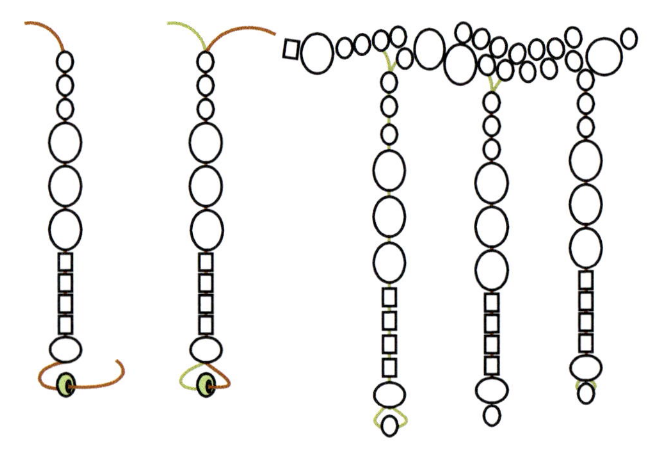

Basic fringe using a single turn bead. Be sure to keep the tension tight to remove any excess beading thread from the fringe.

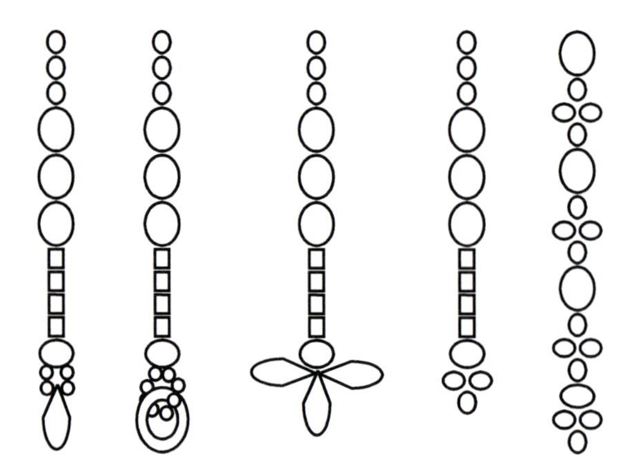

Novelty beads add visual interest to fringe ends, as do simple patterns. Beading through the transitions creates a more polished finish.

Basic Fringe. The simplest fringe is a straight line of beads with a turn bead at the end. String your needle with beads until you reach the desired fringe length. Add one more small seed bead (size 11° or smaller) as your turn bead. Then string your needle back through the other beads until you reach the top of the fringe.

To tighten the tension and remove any excess thread from the fringe, hold the turn bead between two fingers and gently pull on the beading thread with your other hand, drawing the bead up until it lies snug against the bead just above it. Taking the time to tighten the tension and remove excess beading thread from each fringe creates a much more professional finish. Work your needle through the main body of your work to the next fringe site. Either use a doubled thread or stitch through each fringe at least twice to improve wear-resistance.

Fringe Variations. You can vary the appearance of basic fringe by using drop beads or other novelty beads such as glass rings in place of the turn bead. When working with drop beads, use small seed beads to cover the beading thread leading to and from the drop bead's thread hole. A loop of beads looks great threaded through the glass rings you can sometimes find at bead stores. The most important key to fringe variations is to bead the transitions and maintain good thread tension.

Leaf Fringe

Leaf Fringe is a slightly more complex fringe variation. Start by stringing four or five beads as you would for any fringe. These are "trunk" beads, part of the main length of the fringe, like the trunk of a tree. To start the first leaf, string nine more beads. The eighth bead is a transition, bead. Use the last bead as a turn bead and go back through bead eight. String five more beads onto the needle then go back through the first leaf bead. Use the turn bead to snug everything (*see basic fringe*).

Continue adding trunk beads and leaves until you have reached your desired fringe length. Leaf fringe typically ends with a leaf, so be sure to leave space for it if your fringe needs to be a certain length.

Advanced Variations. Some other variations to try include fringe with multiple side branches with their own leaves. Or skip the leaves all together and end the branches with one or more straight tips. This last variation is great for simulating coral.

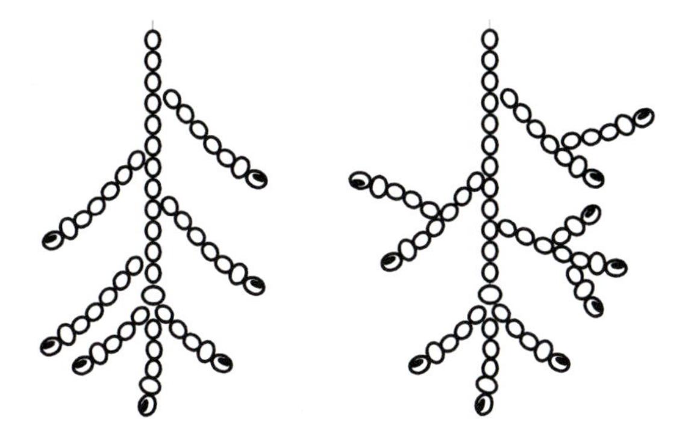

Branching fringe without leaves.

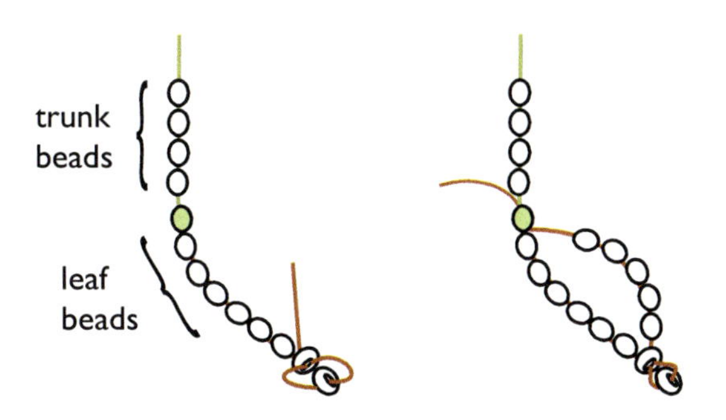

Creating the first leaf. Notice the turn bead at the tip, and the two transition beads at either end of the leaf.

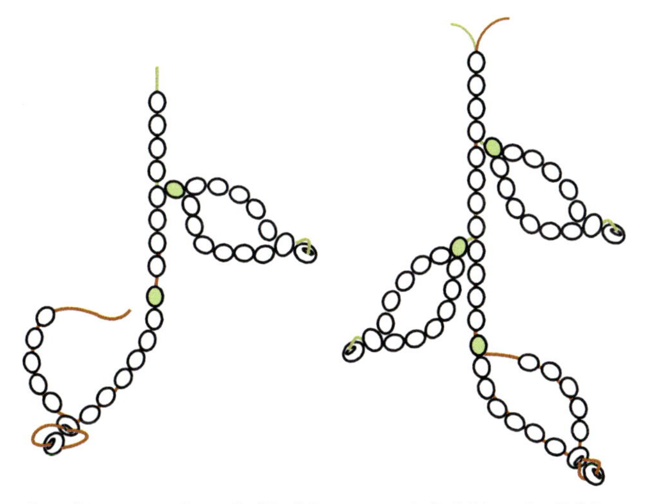

Stitching second and third leaves and finishing leaf fringe. Pull beads tight after finishing each leaf.

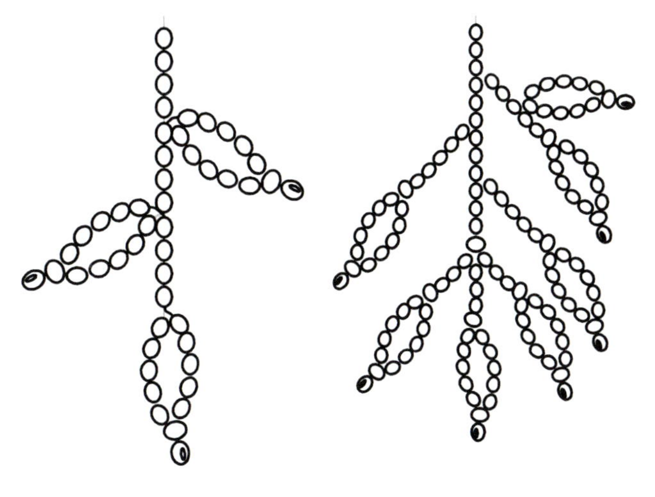

Finishing the leaf fringe. Consider adding "branches" as well as leaves to the fringe.

Finishing Touches - Buttons and Closures

The button closure acts as a strong focal point on the back side of my "Ocean Currents" bracelet.

The closure should be an integral part of the design. I like to use it as a "surprise" or hidden accent. In my initial freeform peyote jewelry, I added the closure bead or button while building my starting row. I don't do this any more for several reasons.

Like fringe, I find it difficult to work around the bead or button during regular stitching – it got in the way and tangled with my thread. Also, I found that the beads underneath the button became quite crowded with thread and I had trouble adding additional beads to relieve the congestion. Because of these difficulties, the button often ended up hanging off the end like an afterthought if I added it too early.

I now build the closure end with clockwise stitching, keeping its width in proportion with the rest of the bracelet. When the piece is almost complete, I add the closure in much the same way as I add popcorn beads; stitching up from the surface of the weave. If necessary, protect the thread with anchor beads leading to and from the closure's anchor points as shown in the diagrams on the facing page.

Your closure will be subject to considerable wear. To help prevent it from falling off, stitch through the anchor beads at least three, preferably four to six times, following different thread paths each time to extend the closure's support.

Above left: Shankless button with beads protecting beading thread. Unfortunately, this button seems to dangle off the edge, unsupported.
Above right: This shank button rests comfortably on its beaded base.

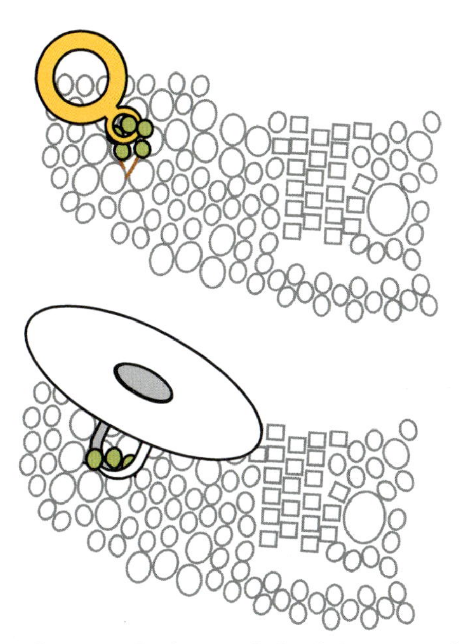

Attaching toggle clasp and shank button with beaded anchor bridges to hide and protect the beading thread.

Shank Buttons and Closures

To attach shank buttons or toggle clasps, run a short beaded bridge through each anchor point. The bridge should be just long enough to hide and protect the beading thread while holding the closure tight. You want as little slack as possible. Stitch back into your peyote base as close as possible to the edge of the anchor point.

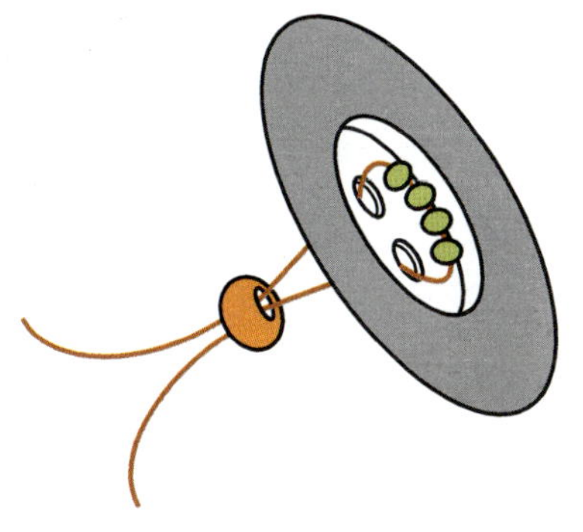

Button with shank bead and beads between thread holes.

Shankless Buttons and Closures

If you are using a button that doesn't have a shank, create one using a single size 6° bead under the button. This is the bead equivalent to thread shanks used for heavy weight garment closures. String the size 6° bead then stitch through the button. Add enough beads to span the gap between thread holes. Stitch back through the button and the shank bead, then into the main body of your work.

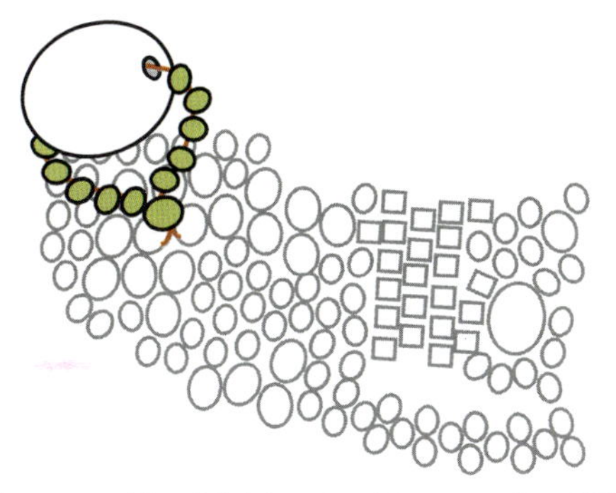

The exposed bead bridges in this example will be subject to considerable wear if used as a closure.

Putting it All Together

Side view of Spanish Dancers bracelet.

I have never been able to count and create at the same time - my brain just doesn't work that way. This is likely why I adore freeform peyote, where I can build my designs bead by bead according to what looks and feels right, allowing the piece to tell me what it needs, instead of by an exact count.

With that in mind, I'll issue a warning; you won't find specific patterns or step-by-step instructions in this chapter - it would impose too many limits on the organic nature of this bead form. You will find pictures, thoughts and notes walking you through my process of creating original jewelry.

Facing page: "Ocean Waves" collar and earrings set.

Ocean Waves Collar

This collar was inspired by a gorgeous chunk of polished sea glass I found at one of the local beaches.

Beginning with the center front, I purposefully left a void beneath where the sea glass would be as I wanted it to be visible from both front and back.

As I worked, I regularly compared my stitching to the mock-up to verify size and placement.

Left: Collar and earrings with the neckline. Photo by JFH. Below: design work.

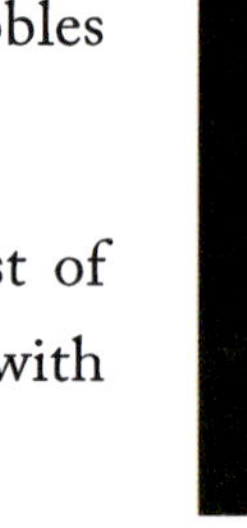

My original plan called for multiple pieces of sea glass. In the end, I only used the single piece as this brought it into even greater focus, though I did use a smaller piece of sea glass in one of the matching earrings.

Drop shape beads in iridescent white, blue-green and turquoise added the feel of bubbles or froth.

The sea glass was added last, once the rest of the stitching was complete, capturing it with multiple bridges and finishing the piece.

Light and Dark Broach

Open and airy, this piece looks quite different from most of my other freeform peyote pieces. I love the juxtaposition of the metal hardware and the lacy bead work.

There's something about hardware washers that I've always found appealing - they've always seemed too polished and refined to relegate solely to utilitarian usage. On a recent trip to the hardware store, I discovered the lock washers, with their star-like spokes, and knew I'd have to incorporate them into a piece.

This piece is all about value - black, white & grey - although one of the greys does have a lovely blue tint. I chose the simplistic palette to compliment the steel washers.

Armed with a range of beads in my color palette, my original plan was to use the four washers pictured at left to create a roughly triangular piece with the lock washer in the center.

Once the design was complete, I added the pin back using bead bridges to protect the beading thread, shown near left.

I began by connecting the bottom right washer with the central lock washer. I decided to create a continuous network or web of beading as I added in the other two washers. That way, I wouldn't have to worry about extra stops and starts during the beading.

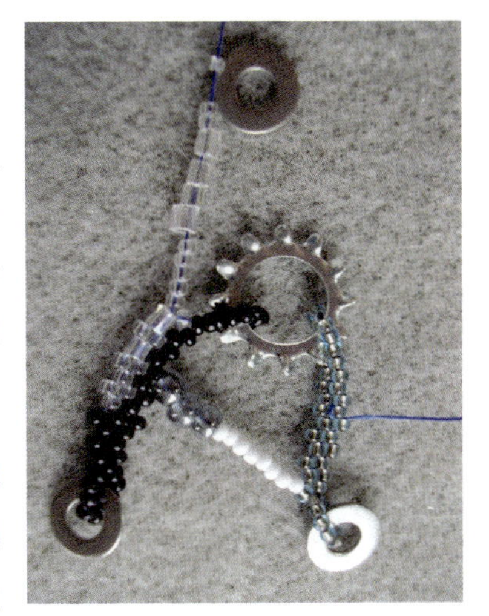

Not far into the piece, I knew I wanted more room to play. I thought to add two more washers, still maintaining the triangular design idea.

The beaded loops at the far right looked like lacework, while the lines radiating from the bottom left washer reminded me of tree limbs. I liked the linear, open aspect of the piece and decided to keep that as the design developed.

Midway into the piece, it was looking good, but I felt it needed something more - some accent to help punch up the design. The black, pressed-glass disc beads were my answer. They were the positive to the washers' negative, the dark in contrast to their light.

The first disc rested on existing beading. But there were no beads where I wanted to place the others. In order to maintain the open, lacy effect I added supporting "nests" of transparent beads which fade into the background (shown in the detail at near right).

Peacock Rings

By its nature, peyote stitch is considerably stiffer along the axis of the rows than along the columns. When stitching rings in the round, this works to our advantage, adding body and helping to shape the ring for us. Don't worry about your starting bead count, or whether it's even or odd - bead counts are flexible!

Both of the rings on this page and the next are from a series I made exploring color schemes based upon a peacock feather. The first ring focuses on the colors found along the outer edges of the feather, the second focuses on the colors of the eye pattern.

Your first circle should fit fairly loosely as the ring will shrink in construction.

Limp and floppy, the first couple of rows will be a little hard to control. I find it easiest to work over one of my fingers so that I can use it for support.

Because rings are so small, I move colors more quickly than I do in other projects.

Stitch through all beads, especially those along the outside edges, several times.

The ring is almost complete in these top two pictures, but I'm not satisfied with how the band segues into the bezel. The transition is rough and awkward; a "T" shape with empty pockets below the 'table top'.

A few more carefully placed beads ease the awkwardness, enhancing the color movement and improving the overall design, as seen in the two pictures directly to the right.

Unlike the first ring, with this one I decided to add a focal bead only after several rows of stitching.

In order to make it work, I drew up the stitching to create one side of a cabochon style setting, then added the other side of the setting after the fact.

To finish, I added bridge work to surround the crystal. If I were to redo this ring, the crystal would be larger the second time around.

Spanish Dancer Bracelet

Originally inspired by a series of experiments with increases, this bracelet is a celebration of things that make me smile - from the warmth of the flame-like color palette, to the ruffled edges that remind me of the rippling sea creatures called Spanish Dancers nudibranches (otherwise known as sea slugs). My goal was an over-the-top profusion of ruffles with enough structure to make it something more.

Looking through my project photos, I'm reminded that bracelets go through a prolonged "ugly duckling" stage. The key is to keep stitching until they leave that stage and amazingly start morphing into a swan, then decide if you're going for swan or peacock. This bracelet went through a particularly long awkward stage, but the final result is undoubtedly a relative of the peacock, or perhaps a scarlet macaw.

Two views of the finished bracelet. Top: front view as seen when worn. Above: full view of the bracelet's right side.

On the fourth row, I start adding increases for my first couple of ruffles. Several rows later, the ruffles are more distinct, although they look rather rough - like I've made a mistake. Note that I'm only shifting colors in the ruffles - I'll blend the colors more as I add additional ruffles.

I completed both ruffles with size 6° accents, then decided to add some size 15° beads in between to better define and highlight the edges.

Now it's time to add some additional ruffles, working off one side of the loop end. I'm working both edges, but only ruffling one right now.

Returning to the middle (detail below) to fill in some empty areas, I added under bridges to support additional ruffles. This center ruffle shades from purple at its base to bright yellow-orange along its outer edge.

A bridge under the original ruffle (above) supports new ruffles (left).

The only beads I'm using in this project are seed and pony beads - sizes 15° through 6°. The physical structure of the ruffles themselves and the color movement through them provides focus and visual interest, inviting the eye to rove back and forth, taking in details.

Bracelet Gallery

Leopard Jasper

This bracelet was designed to showcase a wonderful piece of leopard skin jasper I found at a tiny bead store in Port Townsend on the Olympic peninsula.

The stone bead is quite large, with considerable visual weight. Since it was a bead, I strung it with my first row, but quickly realized that it needed more support both visually and physically to mesh well with the rest of the bracelet. I didn't want to completely block the view of the stone's back, so I used partial under bridges as a compromise solution.

You never actually see the whole bracelet (as seen above) when you're wearing it. Instead, I like to think of it as a series of four vignettes that flow together. With that in mind, I want to make sure there's something of interest from all four views.

Smaller jasper beads, beaded 'strata' and gold bridges carry the interest and marry colors in the side views.

From top: top and bottom views of the complete bracelet. The under bridges help support the weight of the center stone. Three views of completed bracelet.

Hydrangea Spring Bracelet

This bracelet was my first foray into freeform peyote. Looking back, I'm mildly amazed it turned out as well as it did, because I frankly had no clue what I was doing. I'd seen a freeform peyote collar made by an acquaintance and immediately knew that this was a technique I wanted to explore. I couldn't find any books on the subject, but I knew basic peyote, so I decided to wing it.

Remember my warnings about beads with sharp edges? The lovely, sparkly, purple beads I used in the top bridge ate their way out of the bracelet not long after it was completed. I've become a master at repairs, and learned the hard way to protect my beading thread with the clever use of protective beads. The good news? Thread breaks can almost always be repaired, though your design may change slightly during the repair.

I'd choose a different button for the closure if I were designing this now, though the abalone button has held up admirably under wear. All said, there's a lot I like about this bracelet, including the color movement, and the contrast of the bright chartreuse against the cooler blues, purples and greens. I also love the button loop.

Autumn Glory

As I'd already discussed the design and creation of this bracelet in earlier chapters, I hesitated to include it here. In the end, I decided to include it to show the finished piece in its entirety, both flat and as it is seen when worn.

I added the leaf fringe in the final stage of construction, using bridges to tie the two areas of fringe together. The fringe is made from brighter, lighter oranges and reds than in the main body to add to the visual depth, drawing the bridges and fringe even further into the foreground.

Interestingly, the upward bow which is visible when the bracelet lays flat on a surface all but disappears when the bracelet is worn.

Top: full front of bracelet. Right from top: underside of bracelet, front & back as worn.

Hawaiian Shell Fantasy

Another of my early experiments in freeform peyote, this bracelet features a far softer color palette than most of my work.

I'm an avid shell collector, and this piece was inspired by my excitement surrounding my first trip to Hawaii. I began the bracelet on the plane ride to the island and finished it on the ride home. I'd intended to include at least one seashell from Hawaii, either bought or found, hence the name. Somehow that never happened, though I did return with a number of gorgeous shells for future use.

Instead, the highlight of this piece is the antique, carved, mother-of-pearl button I used for the closure, which can be worn front and center or turned to the back as is standard, based entirely upon the wearer's preference.

Several smaller mother-of-pearl beads continued the theme, but this is one of my simpler designs with its quiet elegance.

Left from top: front, side and closure views of the Seashell bracelet when worn.
Left: Seashells found or purchased during my trip to Hawaii, all considered for inclusion in this piece.

Beaded Bead

I've always had a thing for beaded beads. I love the magic of taking a big, boring bead and turning it into something special. I'm particularly fond of the wooden craft beads with the ludicrously large bead holes, which is what I used in this project.

This time around, I left the wooden bead unpainted, something I don't normally do, especially if I'm using other beading techniques besides freeform peyote or intentionally planning to leave voids. But the freeform peyote covers the surface so effectively that the base bead is completely hidden.

I stitched the beaded cord specifically for this project, but decided to make it neutral enough so that I could potentially use it to display other beaded beads or pendants as well. The simplicity of the cord also keeps the focus on my beaded bead, where I want it.

The wooden bead's large center hole made it perfect for this project. By stitching a tubular insert for the hole, I not only guaranteed a very polished finish effect, but gave myself anchors I could use in stitching around the exterior.

With a little trial and error, I discovered that a pencil was the perfect diameter to support my bead tube while stitching.

The tube needed to be at least two rows taller than my wooden bead to make it easier to work with once it was inside the bead. Any shorter and it would be very difficult to stitch into.

Inserting the finished tube into the bead, I started the exterior by stringing several bridges connecting both ends. From there, I worked out from the bridges and around the mouth of the bead hole, focusing largely on one side at a time.

As the first side began to fill in, it was time to work on the other sides. Again, I started with several bridges, filling in around them as I played with moving colors using increases and decreases as necessary to maintain a smooth surface.

If I had painted the wooden bead ahead of time, I might have left voids where the painted surface was visible. In this case, all of the base bead's surface needed to be covered.

To display the bead, I decided to make a beaded cord - using size 15° beads around narrow rubber tubing. I chose the smaller size because the change in scale helped to keep the focus on the beaded bead, where I wanted it. With the size 11° sample, the cord blended too much with the beaded bead, where I wanted the two elements to remain distinct.

Beaded Bead Gallery

I used a blunt tapestry needle inserted through the center hole of the base bead (acrylic rather than wood this time) as the anchor for my beading. In the first picture I've stitched the bead loops at either end and connected them via the initial beaded bridge.

Four beaded bridges quartered the circumference, each with a disk bead centered along its length. Treating the disks as cabochons, I stitched around them, working to keep them evenly spaced.

The disk beads stuck out too much from the first layer of stitching, and the colors didn't work as well as I'd hoped. My solution: adding raised contour lines of beading in blending colors.

My beading forms a skin over the base bead, but isn't actually connected to it. This means the beading could rotate and the center hole become lost if I remove the needle too early.

Planet Three

Top: finished beaded bead strung as a necklace.
Above left: Selection of beads, most 6°, for necklace. (Beaded bead features size 11°s).
Above right: Thread wrapped cord strung through bead hole, twisted with strung beads.

The design hinged on the large, fire-washed, disk beads, reminding me of shisha mirrors from Rabari embroidery. I desperately wanted to use them as the focal point for a beaded bead.

All beaded beads remind me of tiny planets, this one even more than most. Its name stemmed from that association.

Jade and Jet

If you've ever made a beaded bead, you know that one of the biggest challenges is how to anchor your beading to the hard, convex surface of your base bead during the initial stages of stitching.

In my first beaded bead example, I used the beaded core to support the exterior beading. In this instance the base bead had a much

smaller center hole, so that wouldn't work. Instead, I built a loose netting of beading thread that I planned to use as a temporary anchor to start the beading.

However, the blunt tapestry needle I'd inserted through the bead hole as a hand hold proved a much more effective anchor than the thread netting. I stitched a loop of six beads around each end of the needle, connected the two loops with three lines of beading, then added cross bridges between the lines, building up a network of beading. In the second image the bead work moves out from the three lines, forming a rough trefoil.

I designed the bead as the focal point for a wire wrapped necklace. To finish it off, I added coordinating beaded fringe.

Earrings Gallery

Adding the ear wires last so it doesn't get in the way during construction.

Rather than a traditional matching pair, I like to think of earrings as diptychs - each set composed of two related, but unique designs. The three sets featured here reflect that admirably.

Earrings are by far the quickest jewelry to make with freeform peyote. Because they're so small in comparison to other projects, you need to get in and out fast; there's not a lot of room to develop complex designs. This makes earrings both easier and more difficult than other jewelry. Easier for the obvious reason that they're relatively quick to make. But more difficult because you have very little space and time to make them interesting. Don't try to incorporate too many different beads or design ideas. If the earrings will be part of a larger jewelry set, I like to reinterpret one of the more dominant design elements from the primary piece in each earring. This continues to tie the pieces together visually without being overwhelming.

Colors of Klimt

The inspiration for the colors in these earrings came from two separate sources; drawn from design studies I'd made years before while examining the background patterns of Gustav Klimt and from the starkly beautiful landscapes of eastern Washington, dominated by rolling fields of golden wheat and dark blue skies like an Andrew Wyeth painting come to life.

While the blues, yellows and browns relate to both inspiration sources, the sparkly gold charlottes are totally Klimt. Many of Klimt's backgrounds remind me of bead work, made up as they often are by myriad smaller spots or blocks of color.

The palette consisted of seed beads in sizes 11°, 6° and a set of pony beads, for a total of nine bead types, with no accent or focal beads. I'd originally thought to include a dark, chocolatey brown as well, but quickly decided that it was simply too dark for this particular project.

Had I wanted to, I might have tried to incorporate elements of Klimt's spiral designs. While I chose not to play with curves and such here, it's definitely an idea for another piece.

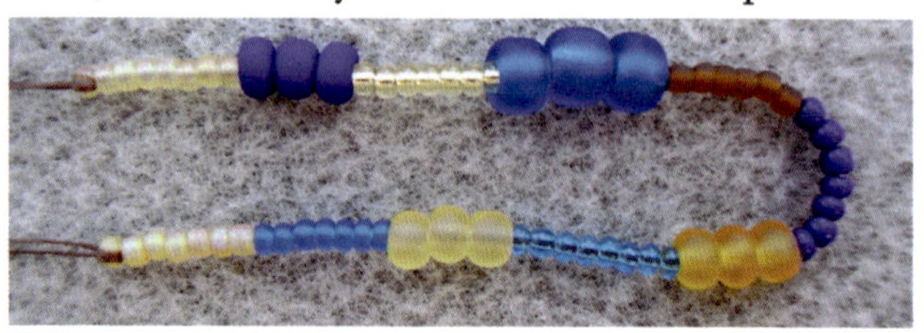

Color test strand, including two types that weren't used.

Right Earring. The starting string for this earring is only 26 beads long - not a lot of room to maneuver! By the fourth row I'm actively moving colors, both the gradual movement of the gold and blue below and the sudden appearance of the lighter blue beads above.

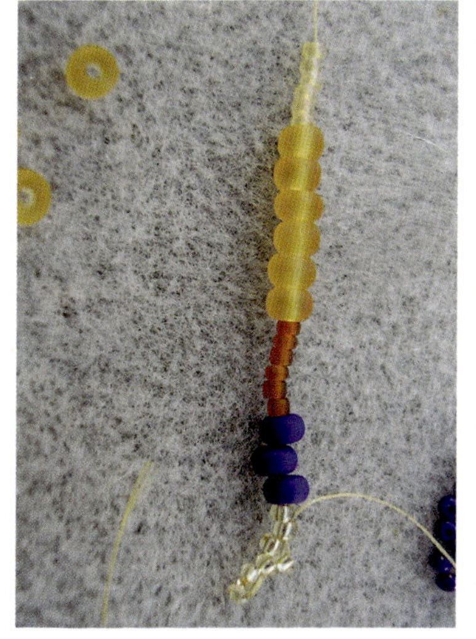

The earring is still an ugly duckling in the third image. I've added another bridge to the lower left, moving the muted yellow beads down and adding bright blue pony beads to enliven the piece. The brown beads are climbing upwards.

Nearing completion in the fourth image, my husband's comment that the bright gold beads at the bottom tip looked out of place prompted me to draw them upwards in trailing lines, like gold dust or corn pollen.

Left Earring. The second earring looks much like the first in its early stages, though bead color and placement have been rearranged. This earring is a little larger than its mate as it took a few more lines of stitching to integrate the colors and design. Thank goodness I wasn't trying for symmetry!

Resources and Bibliography

Bead Sources

Fusion Beads
13024 Stone Ave N, Seattle, WA 98133
1.888.781.3559 or 206.781.9500
www.fusionbeads.com

Beads and Beyond
25 102nd Ave N.E., Bellevue, WA 98004
1.425.462.8992
beadsandbeyond-wa.com

Shipwreck Beads
8560 Commerce Place Dr., Lacey, WA 98516
1.800.950.4232
www.shipwreckbeads.com

Fire Mountain Gems
1 Fire Mountain Way, Grants Pass, OR 97526
1.800.423.2319
www.firemountaingems.com

General Resources

Lee Valley & Veritas
www.leevalley.com
*source for watchmakers' cases (under woodworking: storage)

Nancy's Notions
www.nancysnotions.com
*source for Clover's thread cutter

Storables
www.storables.com
*They have the widest range of sizes for plastic storage containers, including my favorite size for beading on the go

Bibliography

The Artist Way by Julia Cameron. Tarcher, 10th edition, 2002. ISBN-10: 1585421472. ISBN-13: 978-1585421473. A seminal book on creativity.

Color and Fiber by Patricia Lambert, Barbara Staepelaere, Mary G. Fry. Schiffer Publishing (November 1986). ISBN-10: 0887400655. ISBN-13: 978-0887400650. One of the most in-depth books on color and value I've ever seen. Very scholarly writing.

Design is Where You Find It by Orville K. Chatt. The Iowa State University Press, Ames, IA. ISBN: 0-8138-0415-9. This is the book where I had my "ah-hah" moment in understanding the differences between the elements and principles of design, and why both were important.

Beadwork Magazine Presents the Beader's Companion by Judith Durant and Jean Campbell. Interweave Press, Inc. (1998). ISBN 1-883010-56-X (spiral bound). An excellent general reference for any beadworker.

Beaded Tassels, Braids and Fringes by Valerie Campbell-Harding. Sterling Publishing Co., Inc., New York, 2001. ISBN 0-8069-4891-4 (trade), 0-8069-4839-6 (paper). Even if you're not a tassel maker, the beading techniques and ideas are phenomenal!

500 Beaded Objects: New Dimensions in Contemporary Beadwork by Lark Books (2004). ISBN-10 1579905498. Lots of eye candy and inspiration!

1000 Glass Beads: Innovation & Imagination in Contemporary Glass Beadmaking by Lark Books (2004). ISBN-10: 1579904580. More eye candy!

Masters: Beadweaving. Major Works by Leading Artists curated by Carol Wilcox Wells. Lark Books (2008). ISBN-13:978-1-60059-039-9.

Made in the USA
Lexington, KY
31 October 2012